VW Golf Performance Manual

First published in February 2005

A catalogue record for this book is available from the British Library

ISBN 1 84425 101 2

Library of Congress catalog card no. 2004112999

Published by Haynes Publishing, Sparkford,
Yeovil, Somerset, BA22 7JJ, UK

Tel: 01963 442030 Fax: 01963 440001
Int. tel: +44 1963 442030 Int. fax: +44 1963 440001
E-mail: sales@haynes.co.uk
Web site: www.haynes.co.uk

Haynes North America, Inc.,
861 Lawrence Drive, Newbury Park,
California 91320, USA

Jurisdictions which have strict emission control laws may consider any modifications to a vehicle to be an infringement of those laws. You are advised to check with the appropriate body or authority whether your proposed modification complies fully with the law. The author and publishers accept no liability in this regard.

While every effort is taken to ensure the accuracy of the information given in this book, no liability can be accepted by the author or publishers for any loss, damage or injury caused by errors in, or omissions from the information given.

All photographs appearing in this book are courtesy of the author unless otherwise credited.

Printed and bound in England by J. H. Haynes & Co. Ltd, Sparkford

VW Golf Performance Manual

Tim Stiles

contents
vw golf performance manual

There's nothing worse than picking up a book aimed at the home mechanic that is written by an author paid by the word, who has clearly never lifted a spanner in his life. Anything that starts with the words "simply take your air gun and torque to 400Nm" is always going to raise the hackles of any DIY enthusiast.

Happily, this book has been written by someone who likes to get dirt under his finger nails and is never far from a tub of Swarfega – or a racetrack. Tim Stiles made his name on the VW tuning scene in the late Seventies largely due to his enthusiasm for motorsport. After successfully campaigning Minis, the then junior-school teacher decided that he needed a new car to remain competitive at club level rallying,

sprints and hill climbs. The trouble was that the iconic Mk1 Golf GTI was not officially on sale in the UK and so was very expensive. Or to be specific, it cost too much to risk rolling into the scenery…

"No problem", thought the enterprising Mr Stiles, "I'll build my own". Which he promptly did, slotting the fuel-injected mechanicals into a very early Mk1 Golf 1.1 bodyshell – number 303 off the line according to the chassis number. For three successful years this Mk1 'GTI' took part in motorsport events with remarkable reliability. Not bad for a total outlay of £1,500!

To cover the running costs of the car, Tim wrote articles for *Cars & Car Conversions magazine*, with the readers rapidly warming to his down-to-earth style.

By 1985, Tim's motorsport hobby had grown into a fully-fledged business: TSR Performance, a tuning workshop dedicated to all things GTI. Everything from a Mk1 to Mk 4 Golf GTI passed through these workshops over the years, and the company is now regarded as being one of the pioneers of the VW tuning scene. To this day, the company – now owned by Neal Purchase – is still building engines for some of the UK's fastest motorsport competitors.

My own association with Tim dates back to the mid Nineties when I was a humble Staff Writer for *VW Motoring* magazine and was running the magazine's 'Project GTI', a heavily-tweaked Mk1 Golf GTI. While certain people in the VW trade were only interested in selling you parts, Tim was always brutally frank with his advice. For example, I can clearly remember him stating that one modification I had devised was 'just boy racer rubbish and won't make the slightest difference in performance'. This honest approach was refreshing.

So whether you run a Mk1 GTI, or the very latest turbocharged version, you can rest assured that the author has definitely served his time spannering. And if he doesn't know how to make your GTI accelerate quicker, corner harder and stop faster, then no-one does.

Peter Rosenthal
Editor, *VW Motoring*

acknowledgements

My thanks must first go to my long-suffering wife Sylvie, without whose support and excellent coffee-making this book would probably never have been completed.

There are many others, too, who are deserving of my grateful thanks, and these include:

Steve Rendle of Haynes, for his editorial help and guidance.

Everybody at TSR Performance, from Neale the new owner to all our employees, who helped make the business successful.

Geoff Thomas, a great help and support in the early years of TSR.

Dave Pipes for his friendship and hard work compiling the many catalogues.

Dave Trissell, the superb craftsman and head-modifier extraodinaire, whose talents know no bounds.

Brian Rickets from BR Motorsport, whose humour over a pint or two at GTI International kept us all in good spirits, and whose enormous knowledge of GTIs was a great help in moments of crisis.

My long-suffering suppliers, many of whom are family friends now.

Graham, originally from Ansa, who now imports Supersprint and many other products.

Trevor from Koni, along with his henchmen Mark and Gary.

Andy from Kent Cams, always full of helpful ideas.

Chris at Black Diamond for his terrific products and help.

Stuart who imports the superb Schrick equipment.

Phil, from Milltek, for his patience with our manifolds.

Julian, importer of the excellent Eibach range.

Dave, from Autobahn, who imported many difficult-to-get German parts in the early years, but now sensibly sells wheels.

Alan and his family from Jetex.

Skip, because he's just Skip!

Mark at Hamlins, without whose expertise our machining would be much poorer.

GSF for supplying us daily.

Brian Ashley for his manifolds.

Caroline at Magnex.

All the Jabbasport crew for their continuous good humour.

Rick at R&A design.

Jeff at Toyo.

Mike at Quaife.

Petr at Sequishift in CZ for his input with the latest gear.

And finally, though I've no doubt forgotten many, Peter my brother, David my son and Malcolm my friend, all of whom have contributed to our success.

Introduction

Hillclimbing at Wiscombe Park in 'OKU'

After 18 years as a junior school teacher, I started TSR Performance in Bridgwater, Somerset, and it was that big change in my life that ultimately led to my writing this book.

My engineering training had been at Technical College, attaining an HNC, before deciding to follow my mother's example and get a real job as a teacher. As the eldest in the family it was expected that I would become a professional, whatever that meant. However, engineering was in my blood – one of my granddads was a chief designer at the huge Bristol aeroplane works, and the other had been owner of Appledore shipyards many years before – and all the time that I was a teacher I

built and ran competition cars of all types, from a Standard 10 with a Triumph Spitfire engine to many Minis, with quite a bit of success.

I also started writing for *Car and Car Conversions*, mostly on Mini tuning, but later VW tuning in the days of early Golf GTIs. I built and ran a very early 1974 Golf Mk1 based on an 1100 car, converting it first into a 1600 GTI and later an 1800. It was the testbed vehicle for the beginnings of TSR Performance, and it was driven (never trailered) to all the events, and I used it during the week as my own transport.

Eventually I became disenchanted with the way teaching was going, and took the major gamble of setting up my own business with a rented building and the ex-BMC Special Tuning Department's rolling road. This was one of the first rolling roads in the south-west of England, so business was brisk. The highest rolling road bhp I ever saw was a Vintage Bentley of some 8 litres that gave 300+bhp at 2,000rpm! It virtually melted the machine.

At the start of TSR I was on my own, but each successive year brought the need for an extra member of staff, until we reached ten. It would not have been possible for me to have run this business without their support over the years, and I shall always be grateful to them. Our catalogue, which started as a hand-typed and photocopied black and white A4 sheet, is now an excellent full colour job of over 40 pages, bringing in masses of sales.

With the dawn of the Golf Mk2s the options increased, and tuning activities became a balancing act of costs and practical difficulties in an ever-changing world. Today we have rigorous government imposed emission controls and the introduction of ever more complex electronics by manufacturers.

However, compared to some other countries, we in the UK are relatively free to modify our cars, and those of you with the older pre-catalytic converter cars are the best placed. It is important to keep these older cars mobile, as they will command a premium in the future when age and accidents have taken their toll on numbers.

At the time of writing I still contribute to *VW Motoring* magazine. Over the years the questions asked tend to be the same ones, and this book is intended to guide the enthusiast through the mass of information available, covering most of the more modifiable versions of VWs/Seats/Audis, and now Skodas, as thankfully the components are from the same parts bins.

My other love is vintage cars, and I run a 1928 supercharged Alvis. It's simple, reliable and has a huge surplus of power over grip – always an exciting way to enjoy motoring.

My 1600 GTI built-up from an early 1100 Golf, the first testbed at the start of TSR performance.

The TSR Performance base in Somerset is a purpose-built unit.

The expensive bits – rolling road and Bosch analyser.

Rare and rather nice to find – an immaculate original 1100 Mk1 Golf. This one will have a 2-litre 16-valve engine fitted by now.

For those not yet committed to a particular car for modification, the best advice is to look for a GTI model. As well as being less trouble to tune than non-GTIs, benefits include a fuel injection system, a closer ratio gearbox, lowered suspension and more sporty seats and interior. If you have a carburettor car, though, don't despair, particularly if it is a Mk2, as these can respond well to tuning, but expect a penalty in fuel consumption. A carburettor Mk2 will have very long gearing, so it is excellent on motorways, whilst the more sporty GTI has a lower differential ratio and cruises at higher revs and, amazingly, injection cars can return 40mpg on a run, even in quite high states of tune.

The Mk1 1974–1983

The first, and some say the best, Golf was launched in 1974. It is lighter and more agile than its successors and has excellent dynamics. Although a bit noisy at high speed, there is no real downside and it has to be the choice for a motorsport car at club level.

As recommended above, unless you are determined to make hard work of it, choose a GTI model to start from, as all the lesser model Mk1s are lacking many of the most useful features of the sporty GTI. However, with the exception of a variation in engine mounts and

the lack of injection system locating mounts on the non-GTIs, the body shell is the same throughout the range, and with extra effort everything from a GTI can be made to fit, so a really sound non-injection car can form a good base for a rebuild into a powerful injection car.

It goes without saying that you should pick the very best shell you can afford. Condition can vary wildly, and a sad rusty car will cost a huge amount to restore. Watch out for accident damage and badly fitted panels. Try to get a 'feel' for the car – your instincts will generally be right! Remember that pre-1980 cars were not wax injected, and that the early

A very tidy Mk1 GTI still on its original 9-spoke 13" alloys.

I struggled to find this one! It is an unloved 1500 carburettor Mk1. They are much nicer to drive than you might expect and are quite sporty.

The rear of the sill section is often rusty where it joins the rear wheel arch on a Mk1. It can be a sign of serious rust problems.

Sure signs of problems on this Mk1 at the rear of the sills.

Corrosion on a Mk1 door lower edge is not structural.

Below right: A badly rusted area above the clutch cable. The water drains must have been blocked to allow this sort of corrosion.

Far right: The rear chassis rail behind the wheel can rust badly on a Mk1.

sealer VW used underneath the cars tended to trap water between sealer and shell, causing all sorts of hidden problems.

Places to look for rust

- *The rear of the sill where it joins the rear beam mounts*. This is difficult and awkward to effectively repair.
- *The inner wings on early cars*. This area is repairable with care and removal of the front bolt-on wings.
- *Front wings*. These are easy to replace and not worth repairing with filler.
- *Doors and hatches*. Easy to replace but a bit more difficult to find now.
- *The area around the clutch cable*. Look for bodges and cracking.
- *The floor where the rack bolts on*. Look for cracks around the mounts, especially if accident damage is noticed on the car.
- *Around the windscreen and side and rear windows*. Water gets trapped between rubber and metal causing unsightly bubbles in the paint.
- *Rear wheel arches*. These are often rusty, but replacement panels are available.
- *Lower rear and front valances*. It is often just surface rust here, but take a good look at the two areas around the bumper mounting holes for damage.
- *Two box sections under the rear of the car*. If rusted out these are virtually impossible to rectify.
- *Rear damper mounts*. Check for cracking or trapped mud holding water that will have caused rusting under the arch.
- *Fuel lines and filler pipe*. (See injection systems in Chapter 3.)

The condition of the interior will give many pointers to the car's previous existence. Look for torn seats. It is normal for the driver's seat to be badly worn. However, seats are repairable by specialist firms and, except for the centre panels of the seats, the foam and original material is still available. Rear parcel shelves suffer from having excess weight put on them and speaker holes being cut in them. Aftermarket shelves are available.

Without doubt, the most desirable model for the serious collector is the last version, generally referred to as the Campaign. This was a GTI with all the extras factory-fitted. There were only about 1,000 genuine Campaign cars supplied to the UK. European models also existed, of course, and these were available before the British models were produced because the replacement Mk2 was introduced on the Continent several months ahead of its launch in the UK.

Only the leather-bound steering wheel was unique to the Campaign. All the other parts, like the sunroof, tinted glass and twin light grille, were VW extras. Beware when considering one of these cars, as they are not all genuine. Many were built up by owners, and also by dealers wanting to shift the remaining old models before the new one came out.

The Mk2 1983–1992

All the Mk2s are now cheap and plentiful, both 8V and 16V. These are the best cars to modify if

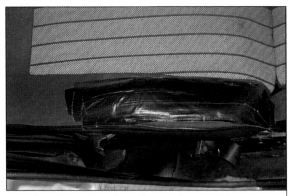

A typical Mk1 driver's seat. If the centre panel is undamaged, it will repair.

you simply want a fun all-rounder car. They are nearly as fast (they weigh more than a Mk1) and still handle really well. They are ideal for taking the kids to school during the week, and taking you for a track day at the weekend. They also have no catalytic converter to limit the tuning potential of the engine.

The 1300s with carburettors are good to modify and, having a low insurance rating, they make ideal first cars. But, for serious tuning look for a GTI model. You have a choice between the 8V and 16V models (the 8V has less torque but pulls strongly from tickover upwards, compared with the 16V which does little until over 4,000rpm). Both are terrific cars with enormous potential for tuning and modifying, I love them! The turbo diesels are only 1.6-litre yet can be modified to 100bhp but, that said, they are not as durable as the 1.9TDI in later cars.

A straight, clean Mk2, a very good starting point.

A really sound 16-valve Mk2.

A Mk2 with rear accident damage around the rear door.

A badly corroded Mk2 front cross member. Only oil-tight engines are normally affected, so it's quite rare.

As with the Mk1 cars, look at the overall condition first. Rust is not normally an issue, except on accident-damaged vehicles, as these cars were all wax injected during the factory build.

Check these points
- *Front end alignment.* Does the bonnet fit correctly, with uniform gaps? Is the crush zone showing signs of a front-end accident?
- *Sills.* Look for damage/rust and careless jacking up.
- *Rear hatch and doors.* Look for bubbles and trapped rust.
- *The front beam.* Look for rust on oil-tight cars and those from places where cold winters call for the roads to be more frequently salted.

The Mk3 1992–1999
The Mk3s are heavier than their predecessors and are less suitable for motorsport than the Mk1s and Mk2s. New legislation required these and subsequent cars to fit a catalytic converter, and this limits their tuning potential. They are excellent motorway cruisers, especially in VR6 and 16V form, and they are much quieter and more comfortable than the earlier cars. It is generally best to avoid the relatively slow and largely uninteresting 1.4-litre cars, unless you are considering fitting a 1.8T 'lump' to wake it up. The 1.9-litre turbo diesel versions are quick, fun and very economical too.

The Mk4 1999–2004
With the exception of the 20V non-turbo so-called GTI, these cars are excellent for modifying. Go for the plentiful and terrific 20V turbo GTI. This car is superb and unbelievable power outputs are possible. It needs lots of power because it has again put on weight, as each new model Golf seems to get progressively bigger and heavier. The chassis is quite a bit better than the Mk3 car, and will handle very big power increases.

Avoid the small-engined cars, but consider the diesel versions as they can easily outperform a V6 version at nearly half the fuel consumption! Diesels have come a long way over the life of the Golf.

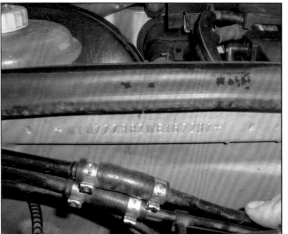

Verification

Before buying, check that your chosen car has the correct log book and VIN number on the chassis. The VIN number is punched into the car from Mk2 onwards (Mk1 has a plate attached to the front panel). The log book should have the registered keeper's correct address, but also check service and repair invoices and MoT certificates to see the car's history. It can be fun and quite revealing. These invoices and certificates are very useful pointers to the attitude of previous owners. Often MoT fail papers are left amongst the documentation, so you can get a 'feel' for the past history of the car.

Take great care with mileages as, especially on apparently low mileage cars, all may not be provable unless the whole MoT history is available to check.

You can get the RAC or AA to check the car (if you want a very long list of possible faults!), but unless it is a newish model the exercise is probably a waste of time. It would be better to take the car to a recognised expert in the model and get an accurate assessment, a service and a replacement cam belt fitted at the same time! Getting an HPI check is definitely worthwhile as it can reveal major issues relating to mileages and crash history.

Safety

If you decide to tackle the modification work yourself rather than employ the services of an expert tuner, make sure you have the tools, the

space, the time and the expertise to complete the work safely. Following proper workshop procedures is vitally important at all times, and one of the most important precautions relates to working underneath a car. Never rely on a jack alone. Always support your car with axle stands positioned in the correct places before even thinking of crawling under it.

Consider the implications of what you plan to do to your car. For instance, the extra power and performance from a tuned engine will call for better brakes and stronger suspension, and the body shell will need to be sound to withstand the greater stresses it will be subjected to. Recording all the modifications you make is a good idea, so that you and future owners can see what was done and when.

Your insurance company will need to be informed of the modifications you carry out. Failure to disclose such information can leave you uninsured. There are many specialist insurance brokers who can provide cover for a well modified car at less cost than some of the well-known big players advertising on TV. You can find names in the specialist magazines, and be sure to get several quotes before deciding. Sometimes you will be called to provide expert authentication that a conversion has been completed safely.

Mk1 Golfs are usually insurable as classic cars at impressively low premiums, and taking out limited mileage cover is another means of cutting the cost of insuring show and track day cars.

02 engine

The 1100/1300 early engine … best avoided. Note the identifying feature of eight bolts around the rocker cover.

It perhaps goes without saying that before starting on your quest for improved performance you need to have a clear idea of what you want to achieve. If, to begin with, you are just looking to improve your engine's efficiency, then 'bolt-on' modifications, such as exhaust systems, air filters, ECU chips, etc., might be all you need for the time being, rather than committing yourself at the start to expensive internal tuning work.

A history

1100, 1300 and 1400 engines

When the Golf first appeared in 1974, the chosen power unit was the 1100cc engine, later uprated to 1300cc. The unit leans towards the front of the car and is fitted transversely across the engine bay with the gearbox to the right-hand side. This engine remained in

production until 1986, so all of the small-engined Mk1s are fitted with it.

The early 1100/1300 units can easily be recognised by the eight retaining bolts around the edge of the rocker cover; the later hydraulic unit has three bolts in the centre of the cover. The early unit was prone to several

The unreliable 1100/1300 non-hydraulic head with long finger tappets and a spray bar.

problems, and these were not rectified until the hydraulic tappet engine became available after 1986.

First, the oil pump was driven by a push fit at the end of the crank behind the front pulley, and this could wear and allow the engine to turn without the oil pump turning too, with disastrous results. It was likely to occur on initial start-up in cold weather when the engine oil was thickest, and thus most difficult to pump.

Second, the overhead cam was lubricated by a spray bar above it which could become blocked with sludge if the engine oil was not regularly changed, leading to very rapid cam finger wear.

This is the main oil leak area on early 1300 units.

Third, head gaskets tended to leak oil at the timing belt end, eventually filling the alternator with oil, and leading to failures.

The terrific hydraulic 1300 engine. Note the three cover retaining studs for an easy recognition point. This tired looking unit has achieved 228,000 miles so far.

These early units are not suitable for tuning work, but are easily and cheaply replaced by the later units. Individual parts do not readily transfer between the two units, so replace the whole engine. They are plentiful second-hand and very reliable, even at high mileages. My daughter's 1300 Golf unit is still going strong even after exceeding 200,000 miles.

The 1986-onward hydraulic units are based on the same block but have largely overcome the early engine's problems. The oil pump is fitted in the sump and is positively driven by a chain, the hydraulic cam followers no longer suffer problems, as the lubrication is more positive, and oil leaks are less likely.

The 1300 hydraulic engine is very similar in design to the later 1.4 injection units fitted to Mk3-onward cars. Little will easily interchange, and care needs to be taken fitting parts from the newer units, as pistons and heads are different – some are flat and some chambered. The latest version is the 16V 1.4, and there are two different versions of this! Also VW built a 1.6 version in single point injection, which when fitted with a big valve head/cam and twin Webers produced 145bhp – ideal for a small-engined car! The down side is the cost of modifying the small engines; they cost much the same as fitting a bigger factory unit, but without the potential of the larger engines. The 1300 G40 is supercharged but was only fitted to the Polo. It appeared as a stop-gap answer for a powerful 1300. It is a very strong and useful engine that will fit Golfs, but is now quite rare. Potentially it is good for 150bhp. No

parts at all interchange between the small engines and the larger engines, nor do the gearboxes or any of the ancillaries.

1500 and 1600 engines

VW realised that a larger engine was necessary, so from 1976 onwards they introduced a 1500cc unit, and later a non-GTI 1600 carburettor unit. These early 1500/1600 carburettor engines were very strong, willing and tuneable. Two different bore/stroke versions of the 1500 engine were made. Although these engines are different from later 1600 and GTI units, they are recognised as the starting point of all the later units, but only some parts interchange. They were single overhead cam, with solid shimmed tappets, and the head was chambered, with slightly dished pistons fitted in the block.

All these engines lean backwards from the centre line of the car when viewed from the front of the car. The GX versions came with a 5-speed gearbox as a bonus, and GL trim, including a rev counter.

When the 1600 GTI unit became available in 1976/77, the block was the same as the carburettor 1600, but there were significant changes internally. First, the head was flat, with valves not in a chamber. The pistons had the combustion chamber machined in a deep dish. The con rod bolts were fitted with nuts unlike the earlier bolt-only set-up. The flywheel was 190mm in diameter initially, but later 200mm on the GTI versions.

These engines are easily recognised by the position of the top water outlet, all 1500/1600 and early GTI models have the top hose coming off the cylinder head between No. 1 and No. 2 plugs. Later post-1986 engines of any type have the top hose exit between No. 3 and No. 4 plugs.

1800 engines

The next significant engine was introduced in 1983, the excellent 1800 GTI unit. There were many changes in this unit from preceding engines. The bore was now 81mm, up from 79.5mm in previous engines. The flat cylinder head had been replaced with a conventional chambered head, the cam was initially a solid

A useful identification point. The lower head is 1600 GTI, the upper is 1800. The water outlets are on opposite sides.

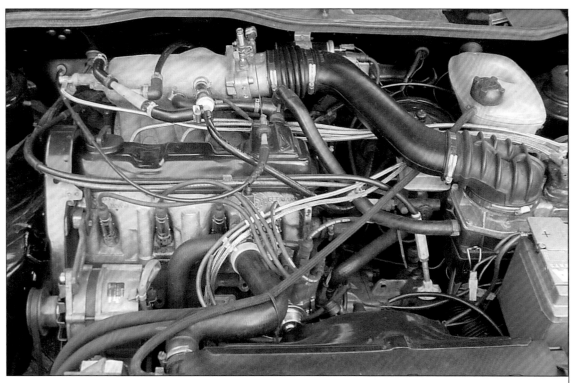

lifter type, but in 1986 this changed to hydraulic operation. The clutch went up again in size to 210mm. With the correct flywheel, this complete clutch assembly will retro-fit to the earlier cars.

The 1986 onwards 1600 and 1800 carburettor engines are very similar in their block spec to the GTI. The bore remains at 81mm, but in 1600cc engines the crank throw is shorter and, obviously, the pistons are a different height to suit. All the con rods are the same dimensions, except that late engines have a useful additional oil feed hole from the big end to the small end for extra lubrication in a critical area.

2000 engines

With the coming of the Mk3 GTI, VW introduced a 2-litre block and a new design cylinder head, like the Audi engine already in production. The injectors fit into the inlet manifold so the head has no injector seats. This head only fits the correct inlet manifold found on Audis and Golf Mk3s – it will not fit earlier cars. However, the block is a good replacement for that on earlier cars, as long as the correct fittings are used (see

section on blocks in this chapter). For the purposes of this book it will be referred to as a 'tall block', owing to its extra height, and not to be confused with the American term for a full engine with a head fitted!

The Audi 2-litre unit, generally referred to as a 'bubble block', was introduced around 1989, two years before the Golf 2-litre engine. It was built to regain the power lost from the fitting of very mild cams and catalytic converters in response to the more stringent requirements of the new emission laws coming into effect in

The 'bubble' block 2-litre Audi engine. This is the same height as an 1800 block.

A 16-valve Mk2 'lump' in its natural habitat.

The VR6 unit is surprisingly compact, and has found its way into numerous converted Mk2s. *(Zöe Harrison/ ZACE Automotive)*

1992. Externally it was different from the 1800 block, with distinct bulges to allow for the longer throw crank which earned it its 'bubble block' nickname. These units are now quite rare on the second-hand market.

The Audi unit is the same height as a standard 1800 engine, compared with the later Golf 2-litre 'tall block' which is actually about 15mm taller than an 1800 block. This makes the 'bubble block', rare as it is, a useful 2-litre conversion on Mk1s and carburettor Mk2s on which you will probably encounter clearance problems with the extra height of a later block.

16-valve engines

The 16V units arrived in 1986. VW had had some early experience with 16-valve engines in French Mk1s built as 16S (*soupapes*, French for valves). These cars had non-VW Oettinger-built heads fitted to modified 1600 blocks. Parts for these engines are now extremely difficult to locate, and they were not really that reliable. VW designed and built their 16V based on the larger 1800 unit.

The 16V was basically a new twin-cam head with 'K-jet' injection fitted on an 1800 block, mildly modified to allow for the external block breather and different distributor drive. The distributor is controlled by an ECU, and is fitted to the cylinder head not the block, so the drive to the oil pump is different. There is a separate drive gear and a blank to cover the hole.

This 1800 16V engine lacked a bit in bottom-end power compared to the 8V units in a normal GTI, so fitting an extra capacity 2-litre block (with its corresponding big gain in torque) to the standard head makes good sense.

The Mk3 2-litre 16V engine has electronically controlled injection and ignition, but as a basic design it is otherwise virtually identical to the previous 16V 1800 Mk2 unit. It has a 'tall block', slightly tamer cams (because of the catalytic converter), and it will interchange directly into the earlier 16V cars to good effect.

VR6 engines

The VR6 was VWs answer to BMW's 6-cylinder engines at the upper end of the market place. The Golf Mk3 had got very heavy, leaving the 4-cylinder catalytic converter equipped car short of power compared with the opposition.

The new 6-cylinder engine was a clever very shallow 'V' unit of 2.8 litres, and with only 15° between the 'V' it allowed a cost- and weight-saving single cylinder head to be fitted. There is quite a bit of engineering compromise built into this engine to achieve the smallest possible package, to fit the limited engine bay space available.

First, in a 'V' engine it is normally the case that if you draw lines through the centre of the bores the crank centreline will be where the lines cross. Not so with the VR6 which has the crank centreline higher than the natural centreline, for reasons of height. This makes the block effectively shorter. Oil consumption problems resulted from this on most VR6 units, especially the early ones, as the pistons get pushed against the side of the bore because the rods follow an unnatural path during rotation. The newer the unit, the better VW have modified pistons and rings to cope with this.

The cams are driven by two cam chains, rather awkwardly placed in the centre of the engine, sandwiched between the clutch and No. 6 bore. Replacing them is tricky and very time consuming. The plastic cam chain tensioner can give problems with old age or excess revs. Early cars suffer from sudden and totally catastrophic exhaust valve failure; it breaks where the valve is joined. They are made from two types of material spun-welded together.

The latest VR6 units are multi-valve, but this is outside the scope of this book.

20-valve engines

The coming of a 4-cylinder 20V unit, with or without a turbo, was new ground in the VW camp. Initially the Audi A4 had this unit, mounted longitudinally. There are many reasons why this is different from the transversely fitted Golf units, mostly in regard to the block fittings and mounts.

The Golf Mk4 brought a 125bhp unit, but then VW added a turbo to make it 150bhp. The turbo unit deserves a book to itself. It's a potent piece of machinery for enthusiasts and an excellent basis for really serious power! The basic 125bhp unit is quite difficult to modify for big power increases, and really no better than the older 8V unit in practice.

A VR6 top lower drive chain. Another chain drives the cams.

Supercharged G60 engines

There are some variants of the older 4-cylinder units that deserve mentioning, as they form the basis for worthwhile modifications. The G60 supercharged engine was an early factory effort in getting the major advantages of supercharging into road cars. The 1800cc unit was immensely tough, very well manufactured with few internal problems. The internals were completely different from a standard 1800 unit,

A G60 piston. The GL stands for G lader in this case.

A G60 supercharged car with a shiny rebuilt Jabbasport supercharger.

with special 22mm small ends, instead of 20mm in early 1800s or 21mm on 2-litre cars. The crank was slightly different, and the pistons were low compression and strong. Heads were virtually the same as 1800s, but were equipped with better exhaust valves to cope with the extra heat produced. These engines were ideally suited to turbo use, too, if the conversion appeals.

The weakness is the actual supercharger. Well maintained and serviced by an expert it will last well. Otherwise, the tiny drive belt will eventually break, causing a nasty bump on the casing and a big pile of broken alloy bits internally. This can happen in an instant and is terminal. To avoid this, get the supercharger expertly reconditioned, including fitting new seals, bearings and belt, every 60,000 miles.

The 2-litre 8V Beetle has brought a superb new crossflow cylinder head with it. This crossflow head is very similar to the later 8V heads and can be useful for fitting one of the superb aftermarket injection systems, as it puts the injection at the front of the engine instead of the back as the older heads did. This gives far more room and makes for easier fitting.

This supercharger is totally wrecked because the belt broke!

Available engines and potential for modification.

(C carburettor, I injection, D diesel)

Size	C or I	Approx date	Potential	Model
Petrol engines				
1100	C	from 1974 until 1986	Poor	Golf, Polo
1300	C	from 1975 until 1986	Poor	Golf, Polo
1300 hydraulic	C/I	from 1986	Excellent	Golf, Polo
1300 G40	s/charged	1989 until 1992	Excellent	Polo G40 only
1400 hydraulic	I	from 1992	Excellent	Golf, Polo, Seat Ibiza, Skoda
1400 16v	I	from 1992	Excellent	Polo GT, Lupo, Seat Ibiza, etc
1500 8V	C	1975 until 1982	Medium	Golf 1, Scirocco 1 carb
1600 8V	C	1978 until 1982	Medium	Golf 1, Scirocco 1 carb
1600 GTI	I	1979 until 1982	Excellent	GTI Golf, Scirocco inj
1600 8V	C	1984 until 1992	Excellent	Golf 2, Scirocco, Caddy carb
1600	I single-point	1992	Poor unless on carbs	Polo 3 rare
1800 8V	C	1984 until 1992	Excellent	Golf 2, Scirocco, Passat, Audi
1800 GTI	I	1983 until 1992+	Excellent	Golf 1/2, Scirocco 2, Passat, Seat, Audi
1800 16V	I	1985 until 1992	Excellent	Golf 16V/rare, Scirocco 16V, Corrado, Passat
1800 G60	s/charged	1989 until 1992	Excellent	Corrado/rare, Golf Rallye
2-litre 8V	I	'bubble block' – from 1989	Excellent	Passat, Audi
2-litre 8V	I	'tall block' – from 1992	Excellent	Golf, Passat, Seat, Skoda
2-litre 16V	I	from 1992	Excellent	Golf, Seat, Audi
VR6 2.8	I	from 1992	Medium	Golf, Passat rare
VR6 2.9	I	from 1992	Medium	Corrado

Notes: *None of the Audi V6 will fit VW's. For Jetta refer to Golf models.*

Size	C or I	Approx date	Potential	Model
Diesel engines				
1500	D	from 1975 until 1982	Poor	Golf diesel
1600	D	from 1982 until MK3	Medium	Golf, Passat, with mods campers
1900 non-turbo	D	from 1992	Medium	Golf 3, Passat
1900 TD1 turbo	D	from 1992	Excellent	Golf, Passat, Audi, Seat, Skoda
1900 PD1 turbo	D	from 1999	Excellent	Golf, Passat, Audi, Seat, Skoda
New 2-litre PDI	D	from 2004	Excellent	Most models

bolt-on modifications

Given the simple fundamental that the better an engine can breathe the more efficient it will become, it is obvious why adding a quality exhaust system, a performance air filter and a really well sorted cylinder head and camshaft is bound to improve things.

Not all the engines respond to the same order of attack, however, and the condition of your existing unit needs consideration. Basically, engines with over 100,000 miles on the clock will be in need of a cylinder head overhaul before extra power can be safely extracted, and this is, of course, the cost effective time to modify the head, as you will need new head bolts and gaskets, etc., anyway.

Air filters

VW generally use paper element air filters in all their models, and most can be replaced by modern high-efficiency foam- or cotton-based filters. The gains are about 2–3bhp. It's virtually something for nothing. The new filters are simply replacements for the existing paper filters, so no skills are required, but the air boxes can be awkward to unclip. Round filters are found in the carburettor 1300 cars but all the rest are panel type.

There are many makes of performance filter, the best known being Ramair, K&N, JR, Pipercross, BMC and Green. Avoid cheap copies with no support for the filter panel, and those with chromed metal support, as I have seen several become very rusty and get swallowed by the engine with expensively harmful results. You get what you pay for with filters.

The panel filters are all quiet in use, exactly as the original was. If more induction noise is required, simply drill a few holes in the base of the air box, it can add a few more bhp too on highly modified engines or early 16V air boxes (up to 1989) as this air box is the same size as an 8V and too small for a modified engine. Do not drill the top of the air box as this allows unfiltered air to be sucked into the engine with the added risk of extra wear.

Induction kits

Induction kits will NOT fit early cars (pre-electronic injection before 1986). Later GTI cars, from 1986 onwards, have more scope with the electronic injection air filter boxes. The air boxes bolt onto the air mass sensor. Complete replacement induction kits replace the original air boxes. These are cone-shaped filters with much greater ability to flow the extra air required by a modified engine. They are quite an improvement over the original units; a VR6 shows 6–8bhp gains with one fitted. They are, however, more noisy in acceleration, but generally fine in cruise conditions. The brackets supplied often require a bit of fettling to get a good support for the filter.

All these replacement filters require special filter oil to be used after cleaning during a service because, unlike the paper originals, these performance filters last for life. Cleaning is done in a shallow oven dish (don't get caught borrowing it!) with either the correct cleaner or

A Ramair panel filter.

A drilled air box to increase available air and add induction roar.

An induction kit for the VR6 from Ramair.

washing-up liquid. Wash the filter well in water afterwards, dry it, then re-oil with the correct oil to suit the filter. Use the oil SPARINGLY; it's easier to use an aerosol than the alternative pot of oil. Too much oil does not matter on non-electronic cars, but any cars with 'hot wire' air mass sensors will get oil onto the hot wire with potentially expensive replacements the only certain cure.

Getting a good supply of cool air is essential to efficiency – hot air is less dense – so make sure there is an easy route for the fresh air to get to the air filter from a cool spot, and try to avoid hot air from the engine bay being the only air available. Shield hot areas from the filter air with an alloy plate, especially on VR6 installations where space is extremely limited in the engine bay. Time spent on this will gain quite a bit of power for no cost.

If you modify any part of the intake, be aware that driving through deep water can allow water to enter the inlet tract, with dire consequences! All VWs can be affected by floodwater, and the best idea is simply not to drive through it at all.

Exhaust systems

Fitting a new exhaust is probably the easiest, and certainly the most popular, modification. Everybody has a personal preference for style of tail pipe and the sound emitted, but remember that the idea that the noisier the exhaust the more powerful the engine is a myth. It's the design of the system that makes it efficient or simply noisy. Buy a well-known and respected system, and choose tail pipes to suit your taste. Be sure all the mounts are included and that there is a warranty. Cheap and poorly designed systems are inefficient.

Stainless steel systems are common now. They are superbly resistant to rusting out, but silencer walls are thinner and thus sometimes noisier. They can suffer cracks too, so check that the warranty covers this. Cracking is often caused by too much movement in the old engine mounts, and to avoid this you should always uprate the engine mounts when fitting a new exhaust system.

Try to keep the same number of centre silencers and expansion boxes as the original if noise is an issue. Taking boxes out has little effect on power, creates a lot of extra noise, and can lead to a failed MoT. The rear box, or main silencer, is critical for power. The best design is a Y-shaped internal path to the tail pipes. Some poorly designed internals simply have two pipes and a sudden change in direction at the entrance of the box. This sometimes shows up in the welding seen from outside the box. The internal packing also affects power and needs to be high quality if it is not to break up and disappear in use.

Some of the most efficient systems are a combination of stainless steel internals and specially treated external non-stainless steel from Supersprint, Sebring or Remus. These are a personal favourite of mine. Jetex make excellent stainless steel systems with all the fittings and they always fit beautifully. Milltek and Magnex have excellent ranges of stainless

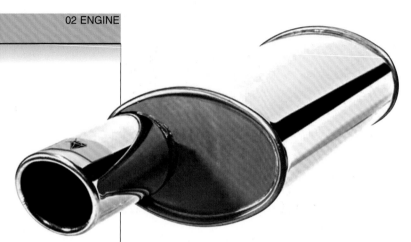

A stainless rear exhaust box. *(Black Diamond)*

steel rear boxes and systems, as do Scorpion. Really, the choice is yours.

Heavy duty hangers are available in factory-spec rubber, rubber with chains inside or poly. The secret is to inspect them regularly to avoid straining the remaining ones! The chain type can cut very neatly through the supporting brackets if there is excess engine or exhaust movement.

Exhaust manifolds

Standard exhaust manifolds are cast iron. The cast is not machined internally at all, so you can get some castings that are better than others. Virtually all these cast manifolds can be gas-flowed to help the gasses escape easier and

Standard (left) and poly (right) exhaust hangers. *(Justin Napper/ TSR Performance)*

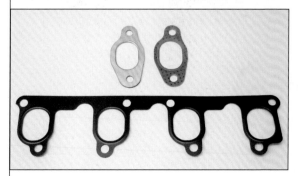

The different exhaust gaskets available, with the best and simplest to fit from the G60 all joined together.

faster. Mk1 GTI cast exhaust manifolds tend to crack, so finding a sound one to flow can be difficult. Some motorsport classes will not allow non-original exhaust manifolds, so there is no choice but to flow the cast one, but nowadays there are aftermarket exhaust manifolds available in tubular steel to replace the most common cast manifolds.

The gaskets between the head and exhaust manifold need to be fitted carefully, as they are sided and different top to bottom too. Many an unwary mechanic has fitted these gaskets incorrectly and tuned away 15bhp! The one-piece gaskets are generally slightly larger in port size, while the composite type are a little more restrictive and tend to squeeze over the port a bit when done up. I prefer the rather neat and durable G60 gaskets as these are all prejoined by a strip so no mistakes can be made, and they also have the largest diameter ports.

There are several variants of cast exhaust manifold, and some are far better than others. All Mk1-based cars, should use the standard Mk1 GTI set-up, including the down pipes. This includes all Sciroccos, Cabrios and Caddies, originally fitted with the disastrous 'ring and two clamps' type. The Mk1 GTI set-up fits as a direct replacement.

Early Mk2s also had a similar disastrous 'ring and two clamp' set-up, but from 1989 onwards the cast manifold improved to the six-bolt type. Use this as a direct replacement. The downpipe to suit this manifold has a sophisticated upper flexible joint well capable of quite a bit of movement on a hard driven car. If looking at buying a second-hand manifold and downpipe, take care as the 16V had a similar six-bolt exhaust manifold but the porting was different so will not fit anything but 16V. The 16V downpipe also has an extra box and is of larger diameter than the 8V one.

Tubular manifolds

Mk1s have a choice of several manifolds (these also fit Sciroccos, Caddies and Cabrios). Some are 4-2-1 and some are 4-1. Both the manifolds from Ashley and Supersprint (chromed) work really well. Always fit heavy duty front and rear engine mounts at the same time for complete reliability and to stop excess flexing of the

Far left: Bad news on a Mk2.

Left: Not bad news on a Mk2.

tubular manifold that can lead to cracking in extreme cases. Also, protect the rubber steering column gaiter by heat-wrapping the manifold.

Milltek make beautiful stainless steel manifolds, available only from TSR Performance, exclusively for 8V and 16V Mk2s, which give a massive power increase on a modified engine of around 8–10bhp. At least fit a heavy duty front engine mount, as the standard mount is very poor and allows far too much movement even on a standard engine with granny driving.

All Mk3 and cat-equipped cars are stuck with the original cast manifolds. There are LHD models available from Supersprint, but these do not easily fit RHD cars because the rack interferes with the downpipe. For racing without a cat, an Ashley Mk2 tubular exhaust manifold will fit if care is taken. Remember that Mk3 2-litre blocks are taller by 15mm, so using a Mk2 exhaust manifold for the shorter block leads to potential conflict with clearances. By

playing with the engine mounts it is possible to fit the earlier tubular manifold.

VR6s suffer exactly the same way. There are no catalytic converter manifolds available for road-going MoT'd cars, but there is an aftermarket six-branch for race cars, and this is ideal for Mk2 VR6 conversions where the converter is not required by law. It has a threaded hole for the lambda probe to screw into.

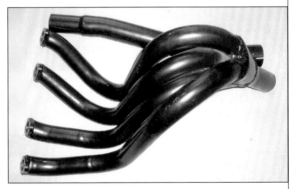

An Ashley 8V Mk1 manifold.

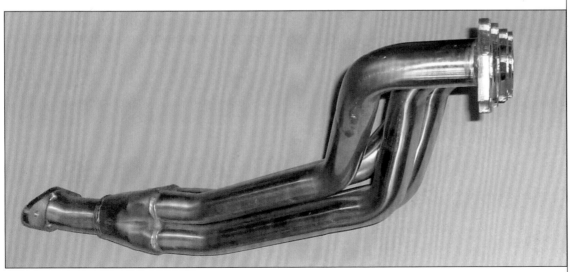

A TSR 8V Mk2 stainless manifold.

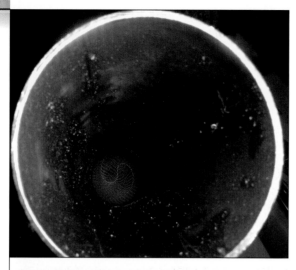

A view into a Milltek performance cat from the exhaust's point of view. The build of the core can be seen.

What you see of a cat.

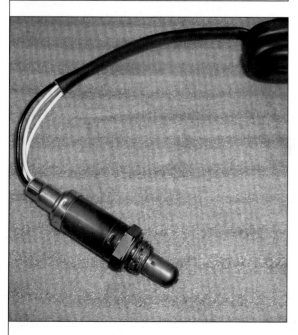

A lambda probe. It is an electronic 'nose' metering the free oxygen available in your exhaust. All catalytic converter equipped cars need one to adjust the fuelling to protect the catalyst.

Obviously, all 1.8T cars have cast exhaust manifolds that also support the turbo, and there are several designs on different age cars. There are no replacements available or necessary. As the cylinder head porting design is not the same as any of the other engines, this will not retro-fit any other units. Shame!

Catalytic converters

It's a sad fact of life that the cat is here to stay. Legislation dictates that on UK cars from K-registered (August 1992) onwards, the cat must be retained. A tiny number of Cabrios were still in stock and they may be exempt if proven to the inspector, but the rule applies otherwise.

A cat is a poor piece of kit in a performance application. It's rather like having a pair of socks up the exhaust at the very point where gas flow needs to be free and efficient. The design has greatly improved over recent years, and they are less power-sapping now than on early Mk3s. They will not survive if they are flooded with fuel, and this is why carburettors were succeeded by injection with ECUs and all the complications, like lambda probes, that the cats brought with them. It's unlikely that leaded fuels will be available for much longer, and when they go there will be one less way to ruin a cat – the lead coats the honeycomb of the cat and stops it functioning. The amount of free oxygen is critical to a cat's well-being, so these engines tend to run weaker (thus less power than a pre-cat engine!), and capacities were raised to make up for this – 1800 GTIs becoming 2-litre and the smaller 1300s becoming 1400s. Fuel consumption increased, too, to the tune of about 10%. So, rejoice those of you with pre-cat cars. Your fuel efficiency will be far better and many more tuning opportunities are open to you, especially with the choice of camshaft.

Lambda probes

The lambda probe is an electronic 'nose' that controls the fuel mixture via the ECU. Engines will only run in 'get you home' mode without a lambda probe fitted, leaving the ECU to guess the parameters. So, it's essential the lambda probe works correctly. They are liable to expire, especially if old or if second-hand ones have been fitted, so get yours tested.

Removing cats

As previously mentioned, all vehicles require a cat to be fitted and working from K-reg onwards, so removing it is illegal on a later car. You might think you can take it off, refitting it just for the MoT, but roadside checks are now getting more common and driving around without a cat will result in a fine if you are caught. For those who still wish to go ahead regardless, there are cat replacement pipes available with fittings that simply bolt or slide onto the exhaust exactly as the original cat was fitted.

Chipping

The ECU relies on chips to control the parameters of ignition timing and fuelling. As all cat-equipped cars run ECUs, the market for alternative chips is growing. It replaces rejetting on carburettor cars.

Superchips were one of the first rechips available, but now there are many firms offering their products to you. The simple early cars, even pre-cat (8V Digifant Golfs), rechip easily, and as it's a fuelling chip there is a good gain, especially on a well-modified car. Obviously, rechipping a much modified car is necessary as the fuelling needs will have changed radically from the factory settings. The 16V Mk2s only have an ECU on the control of the ignition, so there is little gain in rechipping.

The ECU is found below the edge of the off-side windscreen inside the engine bay under a cover. Simply unclip the whole ECU and take note of the numbers on the lid. These numbers are required to accurately establish the ECU type when ordering a replacement chip. Unclip or remove the retaining screws from the ECU box cover, and slide it off in a clean dry environment with clean hands! Remove the top printed board and expose the chip. Pull upwards and replace it with the new one making sure all the 'legs' of the chip are in their respective holes and none has bent over. Replace everything and start the engine. No resetting should be required. Make sure water has not corroded the terminals of the big connector.

Later cars, or those with new ECUs, are far more difficult to rechip. The chip is hard

soldered into the board, so it requires removing and replacing with the correct special soldering iron. This is really a professional job, so contact the chip supplier first. Generally, as a rule of thumb, mid-1992 was the point that this became common. It's really annoying to discover yours is soldered in after buying the chip. It spoils a day! If in doubt, check yours first.

ECU failure?

A simple and very common fault on Digifant cars is the apparent failure of the ECU (the cylinder bores fill with petrol – obvious when you remove the plugs), and it could be that the unit has lost its earth, usually because of corrosion of the earth leads between the engine and chassis. It's common after a clutch has been replaced, where the old earth lead is refitted to a poorly cleaned gearbox casing. The moral is to check yours carefully, as replacement of the ECU is the only cure.

Turbo rechips

The 1.8T units rechip really well, as the chips control more than just the fuelling. The rechip is fantastic value for money as up to an extra 100bhp is possible. The latest REVO units do not require the chip to be removed, and the program is loaded via the port (OBD2) normally used to read the ECU faults inside the car. It can be reset just as easily, enabling settings to be returned to standard for selling!

You don't need to open the bonnet! Simply select the desired program, plug into the port, wait for the tone, and then remove the unit

A 1.8T uprate from Revo.

before starting the car. With the SPS1 program you can switch between the performance or stock (std) programs, and the SPS2 includes an immobiliser which works even if the would-be thief has a key. The SPS3 module has adjustable extra control over boost and timing. This is the future.

Water cooling systems

All VWs have excellent cross-flow radiators, and few overheating problems should occur even in extreme conditions, or high power output situations. The 1100/1300 cars, both Mk1 and Mk2, all have a different radiator from the GTI models. As the engine is totally different from the bigger-engined cars, the inlets and outlets are on the wrong side of the engine bay, so will not easily suit bigger engine transplants.

All the models have a thermostat in the system, mostly in a hard-to-change housing at the base of the water pump. Different opening temperatures are available to suit your needs, but never remove the thermostat completely as the water then does not circulate round the radiator, but instead short cuts via the block and head. The small-engined cars have a water pump driven by the cam belt on the bulkhead side of the engine, so it's hard to get to. The pump has rather soft alloy teeth that can wear badly, so check them when replacing the cam belt. The tensioning of the cam belt is done by

twisting the water pump in its housing, and this can cause two water leaks. First, the housing can leak, and second, the water pipe can crack or simply be corroded where it joins the water pump housing. Replacement is the only cure.

The 1500 and early GTI Mk1s have a radiator with the cap at one end, while later cars have a separate water reservoir on the inner wing. Always fit the later set-up on early cars to avoid water losses from expansion.

All VW crossflow radiators of any age suffer from blocking at the opposite end to the input side; unfortunately this will stop good circulation and require more use of the electric fan. The fan switch is fitted just where the radiator tends to get blocked, so little water gets to the switch at the time that it's needed most! These fan switches are available with different temperature settings. A failure can cause quite sudden rises in coolant temperature with little warning. Replace the radiator and switch to cure the problem. There are two or three terminal switches, so check yours first.

The radiators have alloy cores with plastic ends clipped on, and old ones can be leaky where the seals seep. All water pumps are adequate if they are in sound condition. Some cheap water pumps can lose the plastic impeller if the engine gets very hot at any time.

Always use high-quality antifreeze at all times of the year, as the antifreeze acts as an

A nice new replacement steel water pipe from the front of the 8V or 16V engine. They often corrode badly and fail on all models.

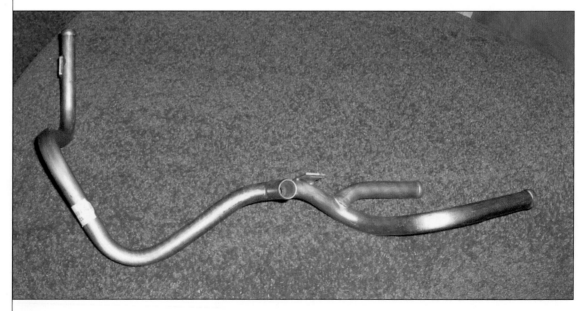

effective inhibitor to corrosion. As the engine blocks are cast iron, and the cylinder heads alloy, electrolytic action can and will occur without the additive. Many early Australian 1500 Golfs were eaten away internally because VWs assembled from kits in Australia did not have antifreeze put in the coolant.

The steel water tube that connects the pipes across the front of the engine can get very corroded internally and is a common source of a sudden and major leak.

Mk2 and later Golfs were fitted with a water/oil intercooler. It was intended to warm up the oil quickly and allow the water radiator to keep the oil temperature stable when the engine is pushed hard. Actually, it is a poor design and can, without warning, allow oil into the water system under full oil pressure. The first you know is a very dirty water header tank, and a lack of oil in the sump, as it's in the water now!

Replace the unit if you are unsure, and don't think it is the head gasket that has failed.

Even VW dealers still regularly get this diagnosis incorrect. I have seen many customers who have been told by VW that their heads are cracked and leaking, when an intercooler was the problem. On well-modified engines, take it off altogether and replace it with an aftermarket oil cooler kit with a thermostat. It is difficult to find room for the oil cooler and the intercooler if you try to fit both.

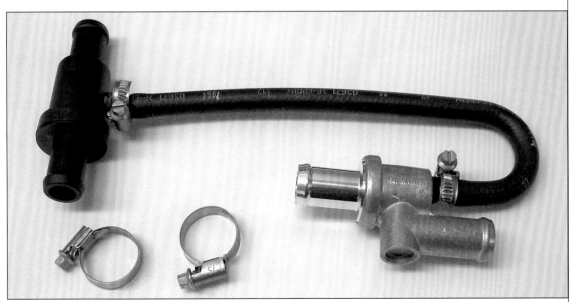

The Mk2 heater core.

A VR6 additional water pump, a common failure point. It circulates the water while the engine is running slowly.

All Mk2 cars suffered from a heater core problem, but there was a manufacturer recall, so all should have been fitted with a VW kit to alleviate this problem. The heater core is tricky to replace. The symptoms of a failure are fairly obvious – a sickly smell of antifreeze from the vents and terrible 'huffing up' of the windscreen when the heater is switched on.

Mk3s and Mk4s have excellent water systems, but faults can occur on VR6s and similar models with the 2-speed fans, usually because of relay problems. The VR6 can also have problems at low engine speed or in traffic if the small additional electric water pump fails.

Silicone hoses are a good investment, as they look great, last a long time and cost about the same as genuine hoses from VW.

Oil cooling systems

The basic small-engined cars have no extra oil cooling, but with the coming of the Mk1 GTI the car gained a proper thermostatically controlled oil cooler. The thermostat and oil cooler pipe fittings are built into the oil filter housing. This is neat and easy to fit to later cars, but the pipe fittings have metric threads, not BSP threads, so you need to be careful to

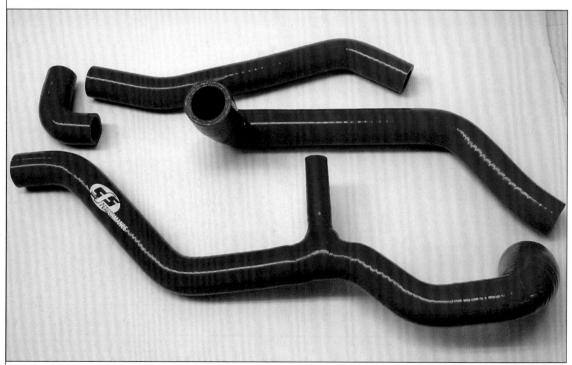

A set of silicone hoses.

A Mk1 oil cooler off its mounting plate. There are two small rubber seals between the oil cooler and the mounting bracket.

get the connections correct. The actual housing will fit all 1500, 1600 and 1800 units. The oil cooler is fitted vertically beside the radiator, which is excellent for maximum cooling of the oil. One problem with fitting an oil cooler to a later car is finding a suitable space to get some air flow through the cooler.

On 'tall block' cars the housing mounts are different from the early cars, so you must fit an aftermarket oil cooler kit. This has an adaptor that replaces the existing oil/water intercooler. It is essential to fit an oil cooler kit with a built-in thermostat, as this regulates the oil temperature at the correct temperature, providing protection to the engine by keeping the oil warm enough. Oil that is too cold is an engine killer!

An added advantage that comes from fitting an oil cooler kit is that you can remove the unreliable intercooler, allowing the water radiator to simply cool the water instead of water and oil. Also, there is extra oil in the system in the pipes and cooler, so oil temperatures are lower anyway.

It is essential to make strong vibration-proof brackets in a good cool airflow. Use 'cotton reel' rubber mounts to attach the oil cooler. It can be fitted any way round, but upside down is not a good idea as it allows the oil to drain if the engine is not running. It's quite easy to move the water radiator over a bit by using the alternative holes already in the front valence to gain room to fit the oil cooler.

Take great care with routing the oil cooler pipes, making sure they cannot chafe on anything, as high-pressure oil escapes quickly

and will spoil your day. Never use old oil cooler pipes, as they crack up internally and can block up the oil system's small holes. You can get new pipes, made to take at least 10bar pressure, or alternatively take your fitting to your local hydraulic pipe dealer and get them to make up new purpose-built pipes. If you suffer an engine blow up, NEVER reuse the oil cooler! It will contain all the missing engine parts in its fine oilways. They are virtually impossible to remove, but have an ability to reappear in your new engine's oil system at a later time.

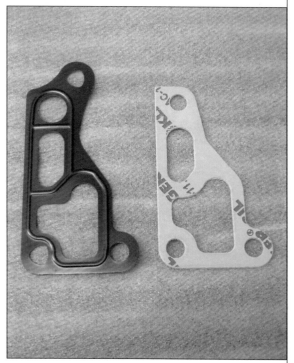

The oil filter housings have different faces and stud patterns. The gasket for the tall block is on the left, the earlier short block on the right.

cylinder heads

All the fuel-air mixture your engine breathes, and then turns into bhp, will flow through your cylinder head – in through the inlet port to be burnt, and then out through the exhaust port. There are three basic designs and numerous different castings. Most of the engines are two valves per cylinder, with a single overhead cam operating them. Then there are the engines with four valves per cylinder, with two cams, each one operating separate inlet and exhaust valves; and there are now five valve per cylinder designs, also running two cams – the three inlet valves opened by one cam, and the two exhaust valves by the other cam. This design is common to Audi and many of the latest VWs.

Why modify the head?

The answer to that question is: Because, by expertly shaping and polishing the ports in the cylinder head, and by making obstructions, such as the valve guides and valve seats, finer or less obstructive, you can help your engine draw in fuel and air more easily, burn it without waste and blow the burnt gasses out into the exhaust with the least back pressure. All of which leads to greater efficiency.

The efficiency of the standard ex-factory cylinder head will be restricted by the limits on the time and money that the manufacturers' mass-production arithmetic enabled them to spend on it. In practice, castings are only machined where gaskets or valve seats fit, and the rest of the internals are left as raw casting.

Some will be better than others, depending on the quality of the casting, but all will benefit greatly from 'gas flowing' to produce a smooth finish and thereby improve the flow of the gasses through the ports. 'Gas flowing' the chambers, if your head has them (some heads are flat), also pays dividends, and the skilled operator can accurately match chamber sizes so that they all have equal compression and efficiency.

All VW heads are of aluminium alloy, fitted with hardened steel valve seats. These cope perfectly well with unleaded fuels, and the valve seats hardly ever come loose or wear. However, the valve guides and seals do wear quite rapidly and any engine over the magic 100,000 miles will need to have both replaced if any tuning work is to be done. Look for excessive oil smoke in the rear-view mirror under over-run conditions when the engine is thoroughly hot. Change down early as you exit a motorway, and look behind you. A big puff of smoke usually means that the engine needs a head rebuild or the engine breathers are partly blocked. There may also be nasty 'pinking', especially if the car is pre-electronic injection, as the oil gets sucked into the combustion chambers, effectively lowering the octane rating of the fuel.

Stripping the head will require a special deep valve spring compressor, a small magnetic pen (to grab the collets as they come loose) and, for non-hydraulic engines, two tools to reshim the

Right: An 1800 standard chamber before modifying. Plenty of scope here.

Far right: A 'Pack A' standard valve flowed head. Note the narrow valve seats.

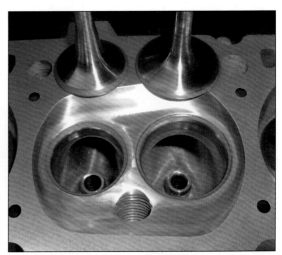

tappets. You will also need a valve grinding stick and some fine grinding paste.

The carburettor cars have heads that are not interchangeable or convertible for fuel injection cars, as there are no injector holes. The cars fitted with single-point injection basically run carburettor heads, as the single injector fits where the carburettor would have been, outside the head in the inlet manifold. All GTIs run the injectors either directly into the inlet port in the head casting or, on later Mk3 onwards cars, partly in the inlet port and partly in the inlet manifold.

The flow through the head (and inlet/exhaust manifolds) is expressed in cfm (cubic feet per minute). A test rig can measure the flow in different situations; for example, with bigger valves or more valve lift. This work is very time consuming and expensive so most people opt for a cylinder head that has been modified by a known expert. In getting this done, the lowest price should not be your criterion. Choose instead a company with the right attitude and a racing background. The best tuners generally run the most successful cars in motorsport, and this is reflected in the road car engines they work on – racing does indeed improve the breed.

You will find that heads are available in several forms. Some tuners call them 'Stages', but we at TSR use the description 'Pack'. The most basic conversion will retain the standard valve sizes, but be fully 'gas flowed' with new valve guides and seals. The second 'Pack' is fitting larger valves, and the third uses special race or competition specification components. As long as the correct cam is chosen, the higher

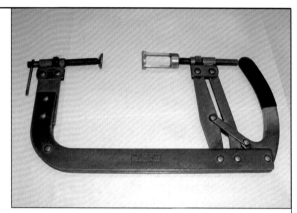

The deep valve spring compressor needed to work on these engines.

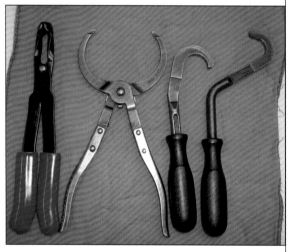

These other tools are only needed on non-hydraulic engines. Left to right: valve seal removal tool, shim removal tool, and two different tools to lift the follower open so the shim can be extracted.

the spec head that you fit, the better your engine will breathe.

Fuel consumption is largely unaffected by this work. Very often, at the same speeds and load, the consumption is far better, as the efficiency of the engine has been greatly improved. Most of us, though, tend to use the better breathing to go faster.

The injector seats. Left to right: early Mk1, hydraulic Digifant, a conversion seat to allow K jet injectors to fit a late hydraulic head, and a Mk3.

8-valve heads

First, the most common two-valve-per cylinder heads are found on all pre-16V engines in one form or another. Starting with the smaller engine first, the 1300 (the 1100 engine is economically unviable for tuning work).

1300

As mentioned before, the 1300 head came in several different designs according to age and model, but the theory is the same. They are all crossflow, with exhaust port opposite the inlet. This is a good design for power and efficiency.

In standard form the valve sizes are adequate. A properly ported and flowed standard valve size can give up to 85bhp with a Weber replacement carburettor, or 100bhp with twin 40 DCOEs. Fitting bigger valves (the maximum is 2mm larger) requires new valve seats, and this is a job for a skilled mechanic in a machine shop. The valves will need to be made up from either a valve blank (unmachined valve) or by modifying other available valves. This is also a job for the machine shop.

We once achieved 145bhp on a race 1300 for Germany with a full race head specially built to run non-hydraulic tappets up to 8,500rpm.

1600 GTI

The 1600 GTI has 38mm inlet valves and almost 33mm exhaust valves in a non-crossflow flat cylinder head, so there is no combustion chamber to modify, only the ports. The valves are longer than those on chambered heads, and have single grooved collets. The inlet and exhaust ports are on the same side.

It is very common to find a crack running between the inlet and exhaust valve seats on this head. Very often it does not affect the running at all, as no water can get into the combustion chamber via the crack unless it is seriously deep. A normal crack will disappear if you fit bigger valves, because cutting in the new larger seats will remove it.

With virtually all the VW heads, what matters most is the area directly behind the valve head rather than port size. Thinning down the casting where the guide enters the port and tapering the guide helps greatly.

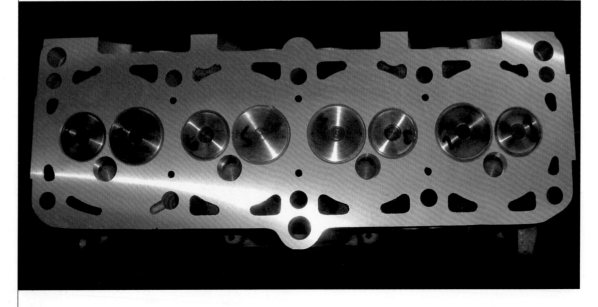

The 1600 GTI flat head with the very common crack clearly showing … don't panic!

A 1600 GTI head with no combustion chambers anywhere in sight!

The width of the valve is effectively the diameter of the seat. This is the restriction the gas has to be drawn past, so open out the diameter of the valve seat, but still leave sufficient (say 1mm) of the seat. The valve only needs a full ring of unmolested smooth seat to close against, not the 2mm flat of the original. Make sure you have the correct tools for this job if you tackle it yourself! You are probably more likely than at any other time to slip and damage the valve seat with the grinder when doing this job!

That final curve behind the valve seat is critical for power. A good engine fitted with a 'Pack A' standard valve head will give 130bhp.

A big valve head requires the fitting of 40mm inlet valves and 35mm exhaust valves. This can give a maximum of 145bhp on the original fuel injection model. The 1600 GTI head will obviously need new valve seats for this, and if you fit bigger valves to both inlet and exhaust, the valve seats need making 'D' shape to allow clearance for the seats where they touch. For road cars, simply fitting a 35mm exhaust valve works really well, as the original is too small.

The carburettor 1500/1600 is rare now; simply fit the later full carburettor engine instead of modifying the original. The carburettor head has very little material around the original valve seats, and it's not easy to fit larger valve seats into it.

1600 non-GTI/1800 and 2-litre GTI 8V
All these heads from 1982 onwards are easily recognised by the top hose position, between No. 3 and No. 4 plugs, whereas the earlier heads have their top hoses between No. 1 and No. 2 plugs from the pulley end.

These heads come in numerous castings, and are all non-crossflow, with the inlet and exhaust ports on the same side, but all are chambered, unlike the 1600 GTIs. Thus the valves are slightly shorter. They are available in solid tappet (lifter) or hydraulic tappet form; the latter having shorter valves to suit the extra thickness of the hydraulic tappet. All the valves have three-groove collets and slightly different retaining caps from the previous single-groove caps. They will not interchange.

A useful identification point. The lower head is 1600 GTI, the upper is 1800. The water outlets are on opposite sides.

The hydraulic tappets will 'pump up' and limit the maximum revs to 6,500rpm, whereas the earlier head will rev to a maximum of 7,500rpm, when fully modified. It is not cost effective to modify the hydraulic tappet heads to take non-hydraulic tappets, but certainly possible.

The Mk3 heads share the inlet/injector system with the same age Audis, etc. This

Superb TSR 40.5mm inlet valves in stainless alloys; the longer non-hydraulic valve on the left and a later hydraulic valve on the right.

On the left are two hydraulic cam followers and on the right two solid ones. The shim (marked '3-10') is clearly visible

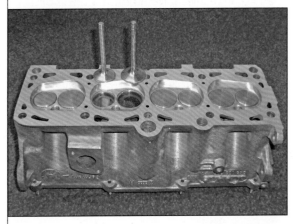

A TSR 'Pack A' head.

The water feed on a carburettor head becomes an injector air bleed on an injection head.

On the left is a one-piece rubber reusable gasket for the later alloy rocker covers, and on the right a cork gasket, with its two separate rubber seals as used on earlier heads with steel rocker covers.

A 4p answer to blocking off injectors if you fit an injection head with Webers!

system will not easily fit an earlier car, so these heads only suit later cars. All these 8V heads produce huge power gains when modified.

Early heads with steel rocker covers have a cork gasket and two separate rubber seals at the ends, but later alloy rocker covers use a one piece rubber reusable gasket.

As mentioned before, the 1600/1800 carburettor heads are virtually the same as the GTI heads, except that the inlet valves are 2mm smaller at 38mm. If you try to fit a GTI head to a carburettor unit, the engine will fill with water! The small hole on the inlet manifold on a GTI (for the air shroud pipe) leads to the injectors. On a carburettor car it carries water to heat the inlet manifold and allow the auto-choke to know the engine temperature. The obvious happens! It can be blocked off if your Weber conversion is running a manual choke, so does not need the water feed.

Carburettor heads have no provision for injectors so will not fit an injection car, but injection heads fit a carburettor car if the injector seats are blocked off and the single twin-choke Weber or 2 x Webers are fitted to replace the injection.

Before modification

Before modifying your head, carefully check the waterways for corrosion. Later Digifant heads seem to suffer most, and the waterway can be eaten away right up to the head gasket ring. Sometimes the head can be welded, but generally it is scrap. As most modified heads are on exchange, check for broken studs and damage, as your exchange payment will not be returned if the head is damaged.

To modify any of these heads, decide on the specification and build your head to suit. An 1800/1900 GTI runs well (135bhp/140bhp or so) with a 'Pack A' head. A 2-litre or 2.1 conversion often makes 160+bhp but needs a 'Pack C' big-valve head to work best, as its air flow requirements are greater with the added capacity. A 'Pack C' big-valve head requires 35mm exhaust valves, but standard 40mm inlets reshaped. The flowing is much like the 1600 GTI.

A 'Pack D', or race head, comes in 40.5mm inlet and 35mm exhaust valve form. Any larger

A beautiful race head ('Pack D') from TSR. This spec head has won the old Slick 50 championship many times, and more recently the VW Cup championship twice, so is very well proven in competition.

than 40.5mm inlet valves (42mm is the largest available) will not flow as much air, because of the shrouding effect of the sides of the combustion chamber. As the valve opens the air gets trapped against the edge of this chamber, whereas with a slightly smaller valve it has room to escape.

Once a cam with more than 276° is used, the hydraulic head becomes inadequate. These cams overwhelm the ability of the hydraulic tappet to cope with the higher lifts and sudden acceleration of the valve gear. This is the time to go to a non-hydraulic head from a pre-1986 car. This will fit any engine but will not work in a Mk3, as the inlet manifold won't fit.

The non-hydraulic heads rev better as the valve gear is far lighter, so up to 304° cams will give a competition car loads of power. There is not a lot of extra power to be gained beyond 304°; the rev range is too limited.

Power output? A VW challenge car, 2-litre with a 'Pack D' head, a Schrick 304° cam and manifold system will give 175+bhp. Pretty good for an 8V 2-litre!

All competition engines running very high-lift cams need the edges of the tappet chamber relieving to give room for the cam to rotate. There is potential too for the shims to be scooped out by the passing high-lift cam, especially at low revs, or more likely when the engine is buzzed into valve bounce changing down too early. The shims are easily pushed out

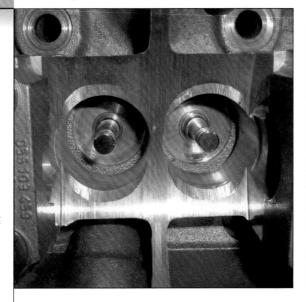

Right: The clearance required for the high lift cams calls for a bit of machining.

Far right: The Schrick VR6 inlet manifold for increased torque. *(Schrick)*

of the indentation in the tappet. This causes the cam to try to run on the tappet directly and usually totals the head!

It is possible to buy a complete Schrick cam kit including the new plain tappets with special shims (lash caps) that live under the tappet instead of above it. They take ages to fit initially, as each one has to be measured then ground on a magnetic table to the required thickness. Once fitted, I have never had a valve gear problem again. Alfa Romeo and Aston Martin tappets can be used with modifications.

If you decide to fit the original tappets to a 304° cam, minimise the potential for this disaster happening by using the thinnest available shim of around 260. This will require

careful measuring of valve length, and possibly slightly longer valves. The thinner the shim, the more likely it is to stay put, and it's lighter too, which helps the valve springs to survive.

The standard valve springs, collets and caps suit all engines and cams up to 7,500rpm, but Schrick make lighter stronger caps and matching springs for competition use. They are superb and well worth the extra expense. A dropped valve is a broken engine!

The cam caps are numbered from the pulley end and must be replaced thus. If you have the misfortune to crack one, any replacement cap MUST be line bored to suit the head. They are not all the same.

All the 8V engines run 8mm valve guides

Right: A Schrick 8-valve kit of lightened springs and retainers to suit a race 4-cylinder, 304° cam.

Far right: Non-hydraulic tappets with the thinnest and thickest shims normally used.

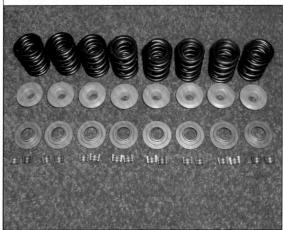

All cam caps are numbered and must be replaced correctly.

Golf heads with an extra cylinder, so modify the same way.

Big valves
Larger valves usually made in durable stainless steel are available from good tuners. When ordering, remember to state the length and number of collet grooves you need.

Breathers and splash shields
The 8V Golf was fitted with an additional oil splash shield inside the rocker cover when the hydraulic engines were introduced. The extra oil supply needed to fill and operate the hydraulic tappets allowed vast quantities of oil to collect in the rocker cover, completely overcoming the original inadequate plate and gauze. The oil was sucked out of the rocker cover by the engine's vacuum and caused huge puffs of smoke behind the vehicle, making it look as if it was on its last legs. It could flood the air filter with oil too.

If you fit a hydraulic head to a non-hydraulic engine, don't forget to fit the shield. It simply rests on the cam retaining nuts. Any modified hard pressed unit should also have one, hydraulic or not.

The rocker cover breather gets very blocked up on older engines, especially if the oil has not been regularly changed. If yours is blocked,

made of bronze alloy. They rarely last beyond 100,000 miles, so replace them before regrinding the valves. Sometimes you will need to recut the seats to suit the slightly different valve guide position. Do not cut the seats more than absolutely necessary, as the last thing you want for power is a big flat valve seat. The more recessed the valve the more shrouded it becomes.

On race heads, fitting a 7mm (16V) valve guide is effective, but special valves with 7mm stems are required to suit.

Audi 5-cylinder units are really 4-cylinder

The splash shield found on hydraulic engines.

Typical high-mileage rocker cover with totally blocked breathers.

How the rocker cover should look.

Below right: An internally polished Mk1 inlet manifold, opened out to suit a bigger Audi throttle body.

Far right: A Mk2/Audi 5-cylinder throttle body; ideal for a modified Mk1, as the secondary butterfly is larger.

replace it with a new one, as they are virtually impossible to clean successfully. A blocked gauze will make for higher oil consumption, as the trapped internal pressure will force past the pistons instead in a bid to escape.

All 8V head bolts must be replaced when the head is refitted.

Inlet manifolds are all different according to the model age. The Mk1 manifold responds to a Mk2 or Audi throttle valve and internal polishing, the Mk2/3 simply need matching to the head and polishing. The Mk2 is better than the Mk1 at flowing the air, as the runners are larger, but isn't interchangeable.

16-valve heads

The Golf Mk2 introduced a new 16V twin-cam head of VW's own design. The company had flirted briefly, and not particularly successfully, with an Oettinger 4-valve head on French Mk1 cars. Their new head had none of the problems that the Oettinger head suffered from.

The 16V engine in the Mk2 has become one of the most modified units we see. It is economical and very revvy, but in 1800 form tends to lack torque. The inlet ports are huge, too large for good low down torque. In their attempt to improve this, VW themselves used a smaller bore inlet manifold on some models – Passat and others. This can be replaced directly with the later 50mm inlet manifold for more power. A small bore 16V manifold (and small air filter box) will restrict a modified engine so that it produces virtually only its original output.

The tappets and valve springs are the same as an 8V uses, but as the smaller valves have 7mm stems and are very much lighter, the head will accept lots of revs and quite radical cams before the components need uprating. Actually the cam profiles are milder with a 4-valve set-up. This is partly an attempt to keep some torque.

You will notice the knife-edged cam bearings in the head, because of space limitations, but the pressure is upwards, and the cam caps are full width. All the caps are numbered and MUST be replaced in the correct order. Pull them down carefully and a bit at a time to avoid breakages of the cam or cam caps. As the cams are pulled down the valve springs will push downwards against the valves that are being opened by the cam fitting, so the tension is far from even. Cams can snap in half if not correctly pulled down.

There is a very good power increase to be gained by gas-flowing this head. The working space is limited in the area behind the valve seats on the curve, so only small grinding tools will fit. It's really a specialist job. Don't open the ports up; simply spend time polishing and removing roughness and obstructions in the air path. Remember there are twice as many components and they are fiddly.

The 16V Mk3 and Seats have a very similar cylinder head. They are a direct interchange

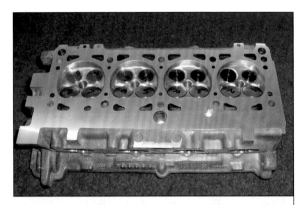

A TSR 'Pack A' 16-valve head.

These two gaskets show clearly the difference between the inlet bore sizes of the two versions of the Mk2 16-valve manifold.

A fully modified TSR 16-valve head.

The stretch head bolts: 8V above and 16V below.

A TSR special stainless one piece VR6 standard size exhaust valve.

15° 'V', so the combustion takes place in the piston crown similar to the original 1600 GTI design.

There are two cams each operating on either the six inlet or exhaust valves. The latest version is multi-valve, with four valves per cylinder. The tappets are the same as all the other Golfs, but all the valve gear is different. The cams are chain driven from the clutch end of the head.

If the head is removed, always replace the exhaust valves even if the standard size is retained. The valves are prone to breaking on the join between the two parts of the valve. TSR supply new stainless one-piece valves in standard sizes to avoid further problems. These valves are lighter, stronger and flow far more air than the original valves.

The head is full of compromise to suit its application. The exhaust is at the rear of the head, the inlet along the front. As the valves need to be over the 'V' of the engine and it is across the car, half of the valves on each bank have long ports, and half have short ports. The long and short ports are totally different in shape and cross sections. Equalising the air flow is virtually impossible, but with a flat unchambered head, there is no alternative but to only flow the ports. This is where knowledge of the air flow in a head is so important.

Fitting the excellent 2mm larger Schrick valves is a worthwhile modification. As 12 new valve seats and 12 valves are required, it is expensive, but power and torque are vastly

between models if required. The cams are milder on the cat-equipped cars, even the odd non-European Mk2 has Mk3 cams! They interchange easily.

A 16V with poor valve guides or bores can allow the breather pressure to build up, forcing oil into the distributor on the end of the cam. Check yours for oil in the distributor cap.

16V head bolts are longer than, and a different shape from, an 8V. They are stretch type so must be replaced with the head. Always replace the cam chain, cam belt and tensioner while the head is off.

There are no commercial big-valve 16V heads available; the standard size valves suit even competition usage. To go big-valve would cost a huge amount for little gain, as there are 16 valve seats to machine and 16 special valves to make. Our 16V Slick 50 car a few years ago ran 240bhp from special big-valve head and race cams. It had to be driven on the road to the events and was hard work!

VR6 heads (12 valve)

The VR6 (and V5) have very clever heads. A single flat alloy casting covers both banks of the

Stretch head bolts for a VR6, note the three different lengths.

improved across the range. Head bolts must be replaced each time. They are far cheaper if bought from Ford dealers for a VR6 Galaxy.

Where the head fits the block there is a small valve, with a ball bearing and spring inside. We have found from experience that it is easily jammed, allowing the oil to 'pump up' the hydraulic tappets at high revs. The engine will miss and the cause is hard to discover. This only occurs over 5,000rpm. The symptoms do not show on the diagnostic machine, but show on a rolling road test as a sudden flattening of the power curve. We always replace this oil valve when the head is off; it's easier and cheaper than having to go back to it later!

A well-built and run-in 2.9 VR6 can make around 225bhp with a big valve head. It's probably the least tuneable of the VW engines, in a cost effective way.

It is far easier to have a friend with you when removing or refitting a VR6 head, as it's too big and heavy to manoeuvre on your own without risk of scoring the head face or trapping a finger. Be very careful with the cam timing when refitting the chain. Turn the engine over by hand with a spanner and recheck it.

20V heads

When VW introduced the 5-valve-per-cylinder (125bhp) head on Audi 1.8 A4s in 1995, it

The troublesome oil valve between the head and block on a VR6.

looked like the head to retro-fit to other VW blocks. Alas it has many differences, especially with the cam belt drive. It is really designed to run with very good emissions, rather than much extra power. This is why it will only give about 10% extra power when it has been gas flowed. The basic casting is well finished from the factory, and is very difficult for a non-specialist to improve on. It looks like a motorbike head internally.

It can make very high outputs; we see a special 2-litre Mk1 GTI with aftermarket injection and wild cams on rolling road days with 240bhp.

A 20V head. It looks the same on turbo and non-turbo cars.

The complex
20-valve head.

VW decided to tune this engine with a turbo for production cars, and this is the form to get very high outputs. The standard 150bhp 'cooking' engine with a standard head is extremely durable and can get to double the original bhp and still survive. The 225bhp version has stronger internals but basically the same head design. Modifying the head will not produce large increases in output but will recondition and make the head as good as it can ever be to suit the chip tuning.

Beetle crossflow head

This head brought the possibility of having a really good modern design crossflow head

The 225bhp
version of the
20V head.

that will retro-fit any 1800 (if you block the second return oil way) or 2-litre 8V engine as long as either aftermarket injection or Webers are fitted.

The design closely follows the existing head design but allows the gasses a more efficient path across the combustion chamber. It also means that there is far more room available for fitting the injection or carburation as it is no longer squeezed in at the rear of the cylinder head between the head and the bulkhead. Another advantage is that the air there is cooler and readily available, unlike the cramped conditions on an original non-crossflow head. Normal 8V cams fit these heads.

All of this makes the fitting a worthwhile job. The standard valves run 7mm stems (as a 16V Golf) and the same size valves as a standard 8V head. It is straightforward to fit 35/40mm valves in their place to make a superb high-power cylinder head even on a road car. We achieved 186bhp on a 2-litre 8V unit on aftermarket injection.

Remember that none of the original inlet manifolds fits this head and the Beetle bits are of little use. You will need an aftermarket inlet manifold to suit either the Webers or the throttle bodies. The exhaust manifold does fit from any 8V car, so at least that is easy.

blocks

Now it's the serious stuff! Having removed the engine, strip it with care and check all the components to see if they are reusable. If the engine has suffered a major disaster, it is usually far better to use an alternative second-hand unit, especially if serious crank damage or oil-system failure has occurred. Such trauma can cause hidden stresses not immediately obvious even under careful scrutiny. A crank that has suffered a bearing failure can weld the shells onto the rod – not conducive to a simple rebuild.

Always try to use matched components from the same block. The factory selects its components initially from the batches it receives from its suppliers, so some of the work is done for you.

The older the engine the greater the chance that it will have been stripped before, and with it comes the possibility that odd parts have been introduced during previous rebuilds. Recently I came across a block with one Audi rod, two early GTI rods and a later oil-drilled rod. Inspection is the name of the game.

Cleaning

Just as cleanliness is next to godliness, time spent scrupulously cleaning the block is time well spent. At TSR it was normal to take half a day on this. Start off with a 'Gunk' type of cleaning fluid. This will bring a normally oily block up like new, but oil-tight engines suffer from external rusting and this is harder to remove – try the stippling guns available to fit in a power drill.

When the block is clean, decide if you are going to rebore the block or not. If not, then hone the bores to give a good finish for new piston rings to bed into. If you have it rebored, either for wear reasons or to increase capacity, then the cleaning will need to be done again with even more care afterwards. During the rebore quite a bit of swarf is produced, and it is extremely detrimental to the oil system. When cleaning, look for corners where swarf tends to collect. Remove the oil gallery plugs and clean them with a bottle brush. Shining a light down the gallery shows up any particles that may still be stuck inside.

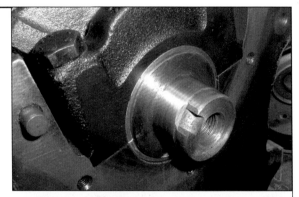

The nose of a Golf crank showing the easily damaged slot that locates the cam-belt pulley.

The cam-belt pulley with a perfect lug. This must be a snug interference fit into the crank slot to survive on a powerful engine with a hot cam.

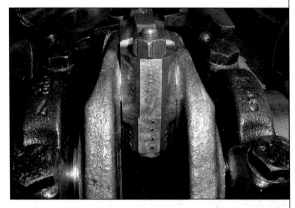

The business end of a crank showing the main bearing numbers stamped into the bearing housings, and the numbered con rod.

Oil gallery plugs.

The con rod bolts that must be replaced every time they need retensioning.

All the modern VW head bolts are only usable once! They are torqued up and then pulled through either 90° or 180° (check the correct block spec for your model) to add extra tension to the bolt. Once they have been used they will not retension again. Many of the other bottom-end bolts are also stretch bolts, and MUST be replaced if disturbed. On 8V and 16V engines this is all big-end bolts, all head bolts and all flywheel bolts (main bearing bolts are reusable). On VR6 engines it is all big end bolts, all head bolts, all main bearing bolts and all flywheel bolts. American reusable bolt sets are very strong and ideal for units that need to be pulled down often.

A professional hot wash tank will move stubborn deposits, and the block dries quickly after the wash. Never sand blast a block, as it's virtually impossible to get the sand out again. Paint the block afterwards or it will rapidly go rusty! Use proper engine paint, as ordinary paint comes off quickly with the heat. A squirt of WD40 will keep the rust away from unpainted areas like the bore and gasket faces.

Take care to check that the head bolt holes and threads are completely clean, as the bolts come close to the bottom of these threads when they are fitted and torqued up, and a bit of water or contamination can cause them to appear tight when actually they are not fully threaded in their holes, which would cause a head gasket failure.

Recognise your block

All VW engines have engine codes, but some new blocks from the factory do not always have codes. This is because the same basic block fits several differently coded models, so it is left to the garage to add the codes. There are several simple ways to spot the engine type without any codes, and a few pitfalls too!

1600 GTI (EG coded) blocks have '1.6' in raised numbers on the rear of the block. Unfortunately so do 1500 carburettor engines, but these are rare now. Not surprisingly, the 1800 GTI and identical carburettor units have '1.8' in raised numbers, but take care, as the same block is used for the basis of the 1600 carburettor unit. As the crank and pistons are

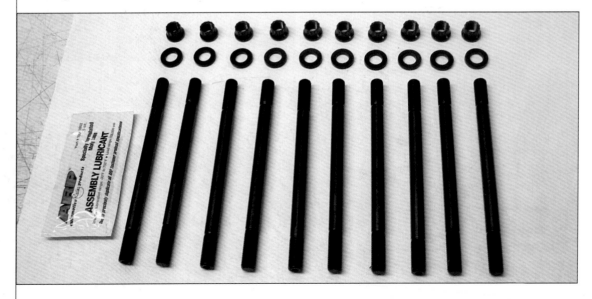

The excellent American uprated and reusable head bolts and nuts for an 8V car.

different, check the length of the stroke before buying it. If it has a GTI head with a raised cast '1.8', it should be an 1800.

VR6 2.8 and 2.9 are identical externally, so engine codes are the only way to recognise the second-hand engine. The 2.9 is larger because of a 1mm bore diameter increase.

The 4-cylinder 2-litre units are found in two forms. The early Audi, from about 1989, has a normal height (same as an 1800) 'bubble block'. It's quite distinctly bubble-shaped, with four bulges to allow for the larger bore. This is an excellent unit for a 2-litre conversion, but quite rare. The later 'tall block' units are plentiful and easily sourced, but require quite a few extra parts to allow fitting into an earlier car. As these blocks are 15mm taller they are quite different to look at. They also have a breather on the front of the block, and different drillings on the oil filter housing.

The Audi models will fit the transverse Golf models, but not the other way round. Golf models will not fit Audis! This is because the engine mounting bolt holes are not cast into the Golf blocks.

G60 blocks have a large hole in the water jacket at the timing belt end, this is unique to this supercharged engine, so it's easy to spot.

20V and 1.8T units are available in several different forms from 125bhp to 225bhp. The only safe way to buy one is by engine code. Beware, as some that were from Passats will not easily fit the transverse application in a Golf of any model.

Audi, Skoda and Seat models are a good extra source of these units as all share the same basic ingredients.

The front face of the casting of an 1800 block.

The rear of an 1800 block.

The rear of a 2-litre 'tall-block'. Note the TSR-fitted temperature button to check the maximum temperature the block gets to for warranty claims!

Far left: A G60 block with the odd water gallery hole unique to this unit.

Left: A 20V bottom-end. It may look like all other 4-cylinder engines, but it is totally different.

Cranks

All the engine sizes have different cranks in standard form, as it's the stroke and the bore ratios that give the different capacities. Very few problems occur with any of the standard cranks as long as good quality oil is used and changed regularly.

The 1300 cars have a very strong crank in standard form. The later hydraulic engines use a properly chain-driven oil pump so avoid the only real weakness of this engine. This unit will pull very high revs, with no breakages, given a suitable head and cam.

All the other cranks are very strong. Many will interchange to give greater capacities, (see capacity increases section in this chapter) and this is very useful.

It would be normal to regrind a crank when the engine is rebuilt. The bearings are available in standard, .25 and .50 undersize, but try to avoid the latter on a modified unit, as the crank is slightly weaker. Always use separate thrust bearings as they have a deeper contact area against the crank. Never use the cheaper one-piece main bearing with the thrust bearing already attached. Rebalance any reground crank.

Up to now, regrinding VR6 cranks has not been an option because undersize shells have not been readily available. This means a new crank if there is excess wear on the existing shaft. However, I hear that undersize VR6 shells will soon be available, and not before time! The 2.8 and the Corrado 2.9 share the same crank, and the extra capacity is in the bore diameter.

VW cranks are forged, with the exception of the 1600 cast carburettor unit, which is easily recognised by its lack of balance counter weights. It's a pity as this would make a good short stroke conversion crank! No special extra treatments are required to increase hardness, unlike other cars. Cranks that have run bearings are often slightly bent and should not be reused, particularly on a performance unit.

If yours is very tired, it is an excellent time to

A thrust bearing. It must face slotted side towards the crank.

A VR6 crank. Note the ignition timing disc at the flywheel end.

Right: An 1800 crank with a drilled and plugged oil gallery.

Far right: A 2-litre crank showing the factory's answer to the oilway problem – different drillings.

increase the capacity with an alternative long-stroke crank.

IT IS ESSENTIAL to drill out the crank oilway plugs to avoid the trapped sludge and dirt from escaping later to 'run' a big end.

Most VW cranks, except the later 2-litre, use a ball bearing driven into the oil way to block off the factory drilling. Behind this ball bearing is a cul de sac that tends to fill with dirt. Some 1.9 capacity increased engines seem to suffer from this dirt, as the different harmonics of the over-bored block dislodges it during running.

The crank will need drilling and tapping to accept Allen key plugs. Once these are fitted, rebalance the crank. In future it will be an easy job to remove the plugs and clean the crank. Later cranks are internally drilled without this feature, thus making life simpler. It is a good idea to get your crank crack tested if there is any doubt about its past usage.

Balancing

All VW engines are balanced by the factory when the original block is built, and it is essential that you rebalance the moving components if any parts are replaced. A correctly balanced crank assembly will last a great deal longer, it will rev more smoothly and will be far more pleasant to drive than an out of balance engine, thereby paying you back handsomely for the extra time and money you spend at this stage.

The crank and flywheel must be balanced on a purpose-built balancing machine, and the rods will need balancing for end weight and overall weight. Material is ground off the base of the rods where the weight is greater. The webs of the crank can be drilled or ground to remove weight. The pulleys also need to be fitted at the same time. The balancing is usually done as a crank assembly. The components, including the clutch, will then need to be reassembled in the same positions; so mark them to avoid mistakes. Pistons are generally very closely balanced when they are made.

Balancing does not add power but aids reliability.

Con rods

Each engine type brought a new form of con rod. All of the different types are perfectly adequate for the job and will take massive power increases without breakages. All have fully floating small-ends, where the gudgeon pin is located by circlips in the piston. For race applications, where extra strength and lightness are required, special steel rods are available. These are ideal for 16V units that can rev over 8,000rpm. 1300 con rods are fine as they come.

The early 1600 engines used a 136mm con rod, this has a 22mm small-end and a different diameter big-end from later 1600/1800 units. This is only used in the 79.5 bore engines made up to 1982.

The much more common 1600/1800 carburettor and GTI rod is 144mm long and has the largest big-end of the later units. The small end is 20mm with no direct lubrication from the crank. This rod remained unchanged until VW introduced an oil feed to the small-end from the big-end, and so fitted bearings with a small lubrication hole and a tiny drilling in the centre of the rod leading to the small-end. This is a superb rod for any performance application based on this block. Many 2-litre Audis share this rod.

The taller 2-litre block brought a longer rod, again with an oil fed 21mm small-end. It looks different with a distinct bump in the

The common 4-cylinder rods: left to right, 1600 GTI, 1800 early, 1800 oil-fed small-end and 'tall-block' 2-litre.

Left to right: con rods from G60, TD1 and VR6.

centre of the rod. It is surprisingly light for such a large rod.

The supercharged G60 has a special rod to cope with the extra stress. It looks like a normal 1800 rod but has a 22mm small-end. The T4 2-litre van unit uses a long type rod with a 24mm small-end. VR6 rods are very narrow to fit the cramped space inside the engine. The last type of rod is found in the 20V units. These are very tough in standard form.

All VW rods can be polished to remove the forging seam marks and to lighten the rod. It is essential that not too much material is removed, and to avoid stresses the grinding must be along the rod not across it. Use a 400 grit to finish off. After balancing the rods, you must get them professionally shot peened to de-stress the material.

The con rod, or big-end, bolts MUST be replaced with new if they have been undone, as they are stretch bolts. They are easily tapped out from the rods, but when refitting take great care not to hit the rod with the hammer. It is best to press the new bolts into the rod in a press or vice. Uprated bolts that are not stretch bolts, and can be reused, are available from specialists. These are generally American made, and best fitted if you intend to take your engine down several times a year, or where the engine is to be revved to more than 8,000rpm. The only breakages I have seen with standard bolts, occurred on rebuilt engines where the old bolts have been reused!

pistons

There are essentially two types of piston – cast alloy and forged alloy. All standard VW engines run high-quality cast pistons with minimal problems, even under very arduous conditions, and very high power increases. These cast pistons are quiet in operation, reliable and cheap to replace. Forged pistons are noisier, have poorer oil consumption and are expensive. They are immensely strong but really should only be used in competition engines, and then only for the highest spec race units.

There are two major manufacturers of the majority of VW pistons: Kolben Schmidt (known simply as KS) and Mahle. Both are originally German. Replacement pistons are available for most of the engines, and come in standard size and .25, .50, .75 and 1mm oversizes. All are set to keep the original compression ratios and are supplied with new gudgeon pins and circlips.

If you have a worn cylinder bore, you cannot simply fit bigger rings, you need to rebore to a larger diameter and fit the piston to suit. There are small bhp gains to be had from a slightly larger capacity after reboring, but major gains call for overboring to a much larger bore size.

The compression ratio on the majority of VW engines is fine, considering the lower quality of petrol these days, and the ability of the later knock-sensor-equipped engines to adjust their own ignition timing to suit the conditions and fuel used. Raising the compression ratio is more difficult and expensive with pistons than facing the cylinder head to get the same results. Raising the compression ratio will give more power as long as the engine does not 'pink' or pre-ignite the fuel/air mixture. Knock-sensor-equipped cars will cope, but it's really easy to overdo it! Once the head is faced, you can't put back on what you have taken off if your engine 'pinks'. Cars in the UK are best with standard compression ratios, but gains can be made on certain models.

Mk1 1600 GTIs have a flat cylinder head and deep dishes in the pistons. The 1600 carburettor engine has a chambered head, so fitting the carburettor pistons with 2mm machined off the lip will give more compression. All the 1600/1800 cars after 1983 and other models are best with standard

compression. The 1300s come with several different compressions – usually 8.5. Fit the GT pistons from a multi-point injection unit for more compression (10.00). The VR6 also has a flat cylinder head, so increasing the compression is difficult. It does not make any difference to the compression if material is faced from a flat head. The VR6 piston also suffers from poor oil consumption and high lateral pressure from the con rod angles.

If you remove metal from the cylinder head, always check you still have sufficient clearance between the valve and piston. With the head built up with cams, etc., reuse an old head gasket and pull the head down using the old bolts (without attempting to restretch them!). Use some modelling clay (plasticine) to show how much space is available. Anything less than .5mm is getting a bit close, so cut a pocket in the piston crown to give sufficient extra space. Your local machinist can do this for you. Remember things tend to stretch at high revs!

Piston rings are available to suit your pistons; they are cheap and should be replaced if you are reassembling a stripped engine. Take care to clean the grooves in the piston carefully with an old broken ring, because if any carbon remains in the groove the piston ring will not seat correctly. Spread the ring gaps equally around the piston. Use a proper ring clamp to squeeze the rings after liberally lubricating them before offering the piston to the bore. A gentle tap with the shaft of a hammer should allow the piston to enter the bore. Take care that the bottom ring does not catch the edge of the

bore as the rings crack easily. The VR6 requires a special tool to compress the rings because of the odd angle that the piston enters the bore.

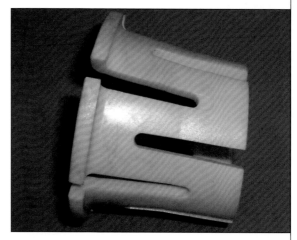

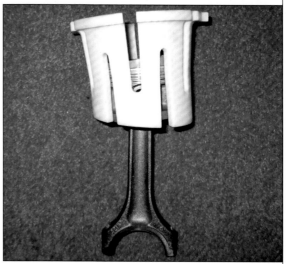

capacity increases

This is a very effective way to improve the performance of an engine, and if yours is being rebuilt because of age and wear it's a good time to do it. As each engine is different, here are the possibilities:

1300

It is possible to go up to 1400cc using the later crank and pistons. The Polo 1600 unit is also suitable for earlier cars, but will require fitting with 2 x Webers, unless you decide to fit all the injection equipment. Also, the twin cam 1.4/1.6 Polo units will fit for a really quick car. You will need to be fairly competent to carry this job out, as it requires lots of fabrication. It's easier in a Polo than a Golf.

1600 GTI Mk1

Once upon a time this was the original capacity increase. We used special pistons and an 1800 crank, ground undersize to suit the small big-end diameters of the rods, to make 1750cc. The pistons are no longer available and, as the later 1800 units slot straight in anyway, it has become less cost effective. As the 1600 GTI head is completely different from the 1800 GTI, the whole engine needs to be sourced, but it fits easily with a different top hose. Mk1/2 GTI and carburettor units are by far the most common engines to modify for increased capacity.

1600 to 1800 carburettor units

The block and rods are the same as 1800 cars, so replace the 1600 crank and pistons with 1800 and it simply bolts together.

1800 to 1900

The 1800 piston is 81mm standard, but 82.5mm/83mm pistons will take the engine's capacity to 1900, still using the standard 86.4mm throw crankshaft. Please read the section on cranks, and drill the oilways as recommended or the changed harmonics of the block from the removal of more cylinder wall, to go 82.5/83mm, will vibrate the debris trapped in the oil way into the bearings, causing a big-end failure. There are no clearance problems inside the block with this engine.

The 1900 units rev well because of the short crank throw of the original 1800 crank, and are a favourite of mine. With a big valve head, etc. they will easily make 140+bhp with total reliability. We have several TSR engines well past 200,000 miles as 1900s still going strong.

2-litre capacity is reached by fitting a 2-litre 94mm crank with 82.5/83mm pistons. The pistons are NOT the same as the 1900 conversion because the 2-litre crank has a longer throw, so the gudgeon pin is higher in the piston. You can't simply add a 2-litre crank to an existing 1900 unit. There is, of course, a readily available factory 2-litre unit, but it needs several parts modifying to fit.

The cranks from any 2-litre VW/Audi/Seat/Skoda unit will fit, except the van T4 engine. If it is from an Audi there will be a bearing in the end of the crank to support the gearbox layshaft. Leave it there; it won't be needed on a Golf.

There are several points to watch when fitting the 2-litre crank into an 1800 block.

Right: The standard 81mm 1800 8V piston on the right of an oversize 83mm 1900 conversion piston.

Far right: The difference of 2mm in bore size shows.

The No. 4 big-end on an 1800 engine has plenty of clearance by the oil pump, but it will touch the block and oil pump drive if a 2-litre crank is fitted, and needs relieving.

The layshafts top to bottom: 2-litre 'tall-block' with the smaller gear, all the rest have the larger gear, but if fitting a longer stroke 2-litre crank, it needs grinding narrower to allow clearance for No4 big-end.

First, as the crank has a longer throw, the oil pump shaft will need machining to clear the crank balance weights. Second, if you loosely assemble the unit, you will see that the No. 4 big-end bolt catches the base of the oil pump mount on the block. File sufficient clearance to allow the crank to rotate, taking care to remove the filings! Third, the layshaft gear that drives the oil pump is smaller on a factory 2-litre to allow clearance around No. 4 big-end. It's cheapest and easiest to machine the end-gear by 2mm on the pulley side of the gear. Carefully chamfer the gear to avoid stresses in the thinner gear that could lead to failures.

On 16V units the oil squirters must be removed and the holes in the oil gallery squirters blocked off, or the pistons notched to allow for the squirters. Oil pressure will be better without the squirters, so maybe that's the better answer.

A close up of the modified layshaft gear.

Far left: The 16V was fitted with oil squirters.

Left: The alternative squirters, 'tall-block' and later engines above, 16V below.

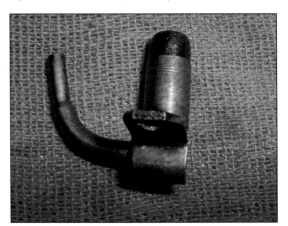

2.1-litre conversions are very popular now, as they are very effective with the Mk3 cars that were originally 2-litre. It does not affect the cat lambda either. Using an 83mm bore and a 95.5 diesel crank increases the stroke to make a lively, very torquey unit. The TDI diesels have a different end on the crank and will need modifying to fit. The normal non-turbo 1900 diesel crank is the easiest to fit.

It is possible to build this engine into an 1800 block, but the crank will most likely touch the sides of the block. They vary a great deal in casting. It is possible to gently grind sufficient clearance without damaging the block.

The biggest capacity we at TSR ever managed was 2.2. It used an 83mm bore with a very 'tractor like' long stroke crank at 99mm stroke. It was massively torquey but didn't like to rev. It was the lazy person's engine – it would pull away in top gear! The crank became difficult to source, so we no longer build this engine.

Fitting a VW/Audi late 2-litre block to earlier cars

The Factory Audis started fitting a 2-litre block assembly to cars to restore the power lost to the catalytic converter in 1989. The unit appeared in Mk3 Golfs in 1992. The Audi unit was originally a normal height block (as 1800s), but Mk3 had the 'tall block'. This was 15mm taller than an 1800. This matters little except on carburettor conversions where the extra height causes the carburettor to touch the bulkhead under hard acceleration. Try to build an 1800 based 2-litre, or find a rare Audi early block.

It will cause problems, too, with tubular exhaust manifolds; the extra height causes the manifold to catch the bulkhead or rack. There are block fitting differences that need addressing as well. The oil filter housing fitting has different bolt hole positions, so the correct housing is required. The gasket is a different configuration to suit, and made of different material too.

The breather holes in the front of the block can be blocked off with a TSR kit of plates. The larger plate has room to allow the fitment of the Mk1 warm-up regulator in its original place, to keep it simple. Reuse the original breather system and rocker cover from the 1800.

The 8V engine has a different diameter distributor on a later 2-litre car. This does not run any advance/retard system that a k-jet injection earlier car would need. You must fit a spacer ring to make up the difference in the diameters of the distributors. If you have a Digifant car, the 2-litre distributor works well, as the advance/retard is ECU controlled.

You will need a spacer if you retain the original exhaust downpipe, to allow for the taller block. These are available from TSR.

The 16V 2-litre units are a direct replacement for an 1800, provided the drive gear and its spring-loaded cover are with the engine, and the correct oil filter housing is used. The breather system has a plastic cover but it directly fits to the original system.

With all the 2-litre engines the head bolts can be 1800 or 2-litre and you need to use a multi-layer steel 2-litre head gasket for

Right: A TSR kit of conversion parts to allow a later 2-litre 'tall block' to easily fit an earlier car.

Far right: Exhaust manifold spacer plates from TSR to allow 2-litre 'tall blocks' to fit standard downpipes easily.

reliability. We have found the cheaper composite head gaskets to be unreliable.

The correct Golf sumps must be fitted to Audi-based engines.

Head gaskets to suit

The larger capacity units need the correct head gasket to suit the overbore. All 1900 or 2-litre units should use a steel 2-litre head gasket for complete peace of mind. They are only slightly more expensive and seal far better than the original composite type.

It is essential to take extra care with a 16V conversion, as the pistons protrude through the head gasket on TDC, so fitting an 1800 head gasket will allow contact on every stroke, causing a mysterious tapping in the new engine. Rarely does it actually damage the piston, but it will eventually lead to gasket failure.

VR6 capacity increases

It is straightforward to take the VR6 from 2.8 to 2.9. Use the Corrado 82mm pistons in a rebored block with standard crank and rods.

The awkward part is getting the 2.8 block bored! Few people can cope with the 7.5° from the centre block. At TSR we had a 7.5° steel plate machined to allow the block to be tilted correctly for boring, but getting the reboring bar squarely into this block is difficult as the head face is also 7.5° from level and requires care. If in doubt, consult a specialist familiar with the engine's awkward features.

To go 3.1 or larger requires special expensive pistons and crank. Recently VW introduced the 3.2 VR6 unit, so parts from this will no doubt be available.

The latest helpful arrival is the V5 oversize piston. As this unit shares many common features with the VR6, including the pistons, there is now the option to fit 82.5mm pistons to both 2.8 and 2.9 units. Good news.

20V capacity increases

The 1.8 20V units have, until very recently, suffered from having few options available to increase their capacity. As the pulleys are different, the crank has a different nose from a normal 2-litre, so the crank would have to be

The later plastic engine breather is different from an earlier one and will not interchange.

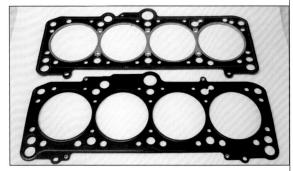

The two head gaskets available. The top one is a composite gasket, and below it is the better steel type.

The difference between an 1800 (81mm) and 2-litre (83mm) head gasket can just be seen.

A VR6 top view showing the offset bores.

made. The pistons have five cut-outs for the valves, but this is always possible to machine into another piston. Since this unit runs a 20mm pin like an early short block car, machining an 8V piston works!

In the United States a 2-litre exists both in turbo and non-turbo types. As this engine gets older, availability of the parts will become more likely at realistic prices. With the turbo engine being so tuneable by increasing boost, etc., increasing the capacity has not been cost effective, but non-turbo cars would benefit greatly.

A 20V crank with the ignition timing ring attached. Most late engines use this system.

The same 20V crank showing the oil pump drive sprocket. The crank is a different length compared to other 4-cylinder engines.

camshafts

Choosing the correct cam to suit your needs is probably the most important decision to be made in building a successful engine. The biggest mistake is to choose too 'hot' a cam for a car used on the road.

First, the theory

The function of the cam is to open the valves, so that the fuel/air mixture can get into the cylinder head and then the cylinder bore. The mixture is sucked into the bore by the piston as it goes down the bore, and the inlet valve needs to be closed before the piston goes back up the bore, or the mixture will escape. After combustion of the mixture, the exhaust valve needs to be open at the correct time, for the piston to push the burnt gasses out into the exhaust system.

The amount of time the valve is open, and how far it is open, will dictate the characteristics of the engine. The extent of its opening is called the 'lift' and it is measured in mm (or inches in the States). There are many reasons why this has to be limited: contact between piston and valve at TDC, valve spring 'crush' (where the spring comes up solid as there is insufficient room for more lift) and the acceleration of the valve are but three potential problems.

The time that the valve is open is called the 'duration' and this is measured in degrees. The duration is also critical. If it is open too long, then the gas will escape from whence it came; too short a duration will prevent enough mixture being drawn into the combustion chamber.

Considerable compromise is made and a great deal of time and money spent by manufacturers in designing a camshaft. Basic standard cars have mild cams, while performance cams can have much more vigorous lift and duration profiles. The longer the duration and higher the lift of a cam, the harder the unit will be to drive in traffic, and the higher will be the emissions. An 8V unit will support a hotter cam (longer duration and lift) than a multi-valve unit, 16V or 20V.

The coming of the catalytic converter has severely limited the choices, so those of you with non-cat cars can rejoice. Cats are destroyed by neat unburnt fuel, so long duration cams are not suitable for these cars. That is why the cat-equipped cars have electronic control of their mixtures, so that the cat is safe from flooding. Long duration cams are not suitable with cat cars, but a bit of extra lift works fine.

Most cams are advertised by duration and, as a rule of thumb, a standard factory cam is around 230°; it will have a very mild profile, but be suitable for all drivers, excellent on emission tests and gentle with the valve gear.

As a guide, do not exceed these duration figures with a road going car:

Non cat-equipped
8V 285°
16V 268°
Cat-equipped
8V 260°
16V 248°

If you go further with the duration, then you are likely to have problems with emissions and tick-over, and the vehicle becomes less suitable as a road car.

Non-hydraulic and hydraulic cams

All earlier Golfs, Mk1 and Mk2 had non-hydraulic cams, referred to as 'solid' cams. The cam followers or lifters had manual adjustment to set the valve clearance. Golf 1100/1300s up to 1986 were all solid, then thankfully the factory redesigned the cylinder head completely to take hydraulic cam followers. The two will not interchange. The early set-up was unreliable (suffering from high wear if the oil was not changed regularly or the spray bar was blocked) and is totally unsuitable for modification. The 1986-onward units, on the other hand, are strong and excellent to modify. The whole engine will swap over easily, so all is not lost. It is not possible to swap early cams or heads alone for later hydraulic parts.

The Golf 1500, 1600 and 1800 units are suitable for cam modification. All these Golfs up to 1986 also had solid lifter cams. The Mk1 GTI 1600 had the best standard cam profile for road use; the later cams in the 1800 were milder. All solid lifter cams will interchange, but not with hydraulic profiles.

After 1986, the hydraulic cam cars had a plastic splash shield fitted inside the rocker cover to avoid huge quantities of oil flooding the breather pipe. It can be a good way of spotting which unit you have, if you are not sure. Many older cars have later engines fitted, so there is often plenty of doubt!

With the rocker cover off, the second way to spot a hydraulic cam car is the lack of a supporting pillar. Hydraulic cam cars have four pillars, not five as the older solid follower cars had. (Some Audis have hydraulic cams and still have five pillars.)

If you have the cams out on the bench, check the diameter of the base circle, a hydraulic cam has a smaller base circle, as the follower is deeper.

It is possible to fit hydraulic cars with non-hydraulic cams, but the valves are a different

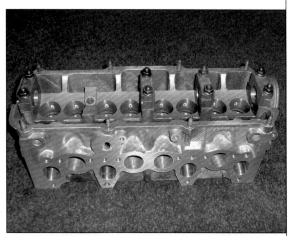

The hydraulic heads have four cam retaining pillars.

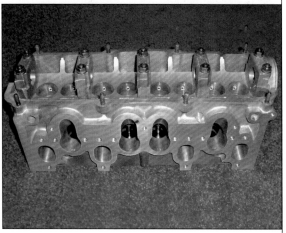

A Mk3 head has different inlet ports to suit the later manifold. This is a rare Audi hydraulic head with five pillars. On a Mk3 the injectors sit half in the inlet manifold not the head.

The complex
20V head.

length and it's not really worthwhile. It's more sensible to swap the complete cylinder head with all the hydraulic parts.

All 16V engines have two hydraulic cams. The profiles of these cams are mild, and even milder if they are cat-equipped later cars. For example, the 1800 16V in the UK was 139bhp, but in cat form in the States the cams were milder and gave 129bhp. That's why the later Golf 3 and Seat Cupra were built as a 2-litre, to make up in capacity increases for the low power from cat-equipped cars with very mild cams.

VR6s have two hydraulic cams, in a single head casting. The 20V engines also run two hydraulic cams, with clever design to run five valves from two cams.

Cam suppliers

In the UK there are several suppliers. Online imports German-made Schrick cams. These are top of the range ultra high quality and extremely well-proven cams, with a huge range to suit every possible application. Schrick also supply complete cam kits, with valve springs, top caps and cam followers according to the kit chosen. Their race 8V cam kit has been fitted in all our TSR Performance championship winning cars for over ten years of motorsport. Schrick make the cams for Formula 1 cars too.

The British cam manufacturers are Piper and Kent Cams. Both make many suitable cams for all models of Golf. Most VW sports cams are made on new castings called blanks. Some profiles can be made from used second-hand cams by regrinding to a smaller base circle. There is a very great saving in financial terms by doing this, as you are not buying a new blank to start from, but the profiles are limited by the amount of available metal on the high point of an existing cam. It is possible to re-profile a solid lifter Mk1 cam to suit a later performance hydraulic lifter engine, as it runs a smaller base circle anyway.

TSR Performance has a range of specialist cams designed over many years for the most popular 8V and 16V engines. Of particular note is the TSR 204 hydraulic cam exclusively designed for cat-equipped cars.

When ordering your cam, make sure you know its advantages and limitations. If you don't know, ask the suppliers for help.

G60 supercharged engines will only really benefit from cam changes as a last option, after head work, exhaust and chipping. Even then, the hydraulic cam is best at about 256°. Schrick make an ideal cam for this engine.

8V cam replacements

You can expect about 6–10bhp improvement with just a cam change, and obviously even better results can be obtained when the cam is fitted in a modified cylinder head.

Remove the clutch cover circular bung and get the engine on TDC. Be careful you have chosen the correct mark on the flywheel, as there is also an ignition timing mark. If in doubt, consult your Haynes Manual! With the rocker cover and splash shield (if fitted) removed, No.1 cylinder (nearest the cam belt) cam lobes should be pointing at 10 o'clock and 2 o'clock. With the distributor cap removed, check the rotor arm points towards the mark on the edge of the distributor body.

Loosen the cam belt tensioner, and slip the cam belt off the cam pulley. Remove the cam caps equally with care as it is possible to crack them if all the strain of the valve springs is left on one cam cap. Undo the cam pulley bolt by carefully holding the cam, wrapped in a rag to protect it, in a vice. Refit the key in the new cams keyway, fit a new oil seal and reassemble the cam pulley.

Replace the cam followers if fitted with a hydraulic cam, as it's false economy not to replace the followers at this time. Old followers will ruin a new cam in seconds. It is essential that the follower's surface is absolutely flat.

Solid lifter followers do not need replacing as you will be fitting new shims instead. You will need two specialist tools and some patience to reshim an early solid lifter cam (see picture on page 35).

Refit the cam to the engine after covering the new cam followers with plenty of either cam lube or engine oil. The cam caps are numbered and MUST be replaced in the original order. Be careful pulling down the cam against the tension of the valve springs; gradually pull all the cam caps down until the cam is seated correctly.

Replace the new cam belt and retime the engine. It will be far more accurate if a 360 degree protractor is used, taking the timing information from the cam manufacturers specification.

Take care to turn the engine over a couple of turns with a spanner on the crank pulley and recheck the settings, before you attempt to crank it over to start it. Bent valves are not cheap to replace.

An essential circular protractor for cam timing.

When you start the engine, do not let it tick over but run it at 2,000rpm for a few minutes to avoid scuffing the cam. The idea is to get the oil moving and up to temperature quickly.

16V cam replacements

Replacing the cams on a 16V engine should not be considered unless the cylinder head has first been gas-flowed. Cat-equipped cars will immediately benefit from simply replacing the inlet cam with a standard non-cat 1800 16V cam. It is a direct replacement.

Remove the plastic clutch cover bung. Rotate the engine until it is on TDC. Remove the inlet manifold from the lower shorter section, and remove the rocker cover.

Check that the No. 1 cam lobes are facing 10 o'clock and 2 o'clock, and then loosen the cam belt tensioner. Remove the distributor from the head, and loosen the cam caps equally in order to remove the cams

With the cams out, sometimes the sprocket wheels need removing to fit onto the

A 16V cam chain vernier-adjustable sprocket wheel.

replacement cams. The sprockets are very shallow, so they look worn out. Don't worry; they are like that from new.

Refit the sprocket wheels and replace the small cam chain. Take great care to line up the two marks on the cam chain sprockets; it's not easy to judge. Refit the cam caps in equal order, and pull the cams down very gently to avoid cracking them. Check the marks on the cam chain tensioners again!

Refit the distributor and cam belt. Use the standard timing marks. Reset the ignition timing in the correct way. Turn the engine over a couple of turns and carefully recheck the timing marks. Replace the rocker cover and the inlet manifold, and run the engine up to temperature. Check the mixture on a gas analyser.

Cat-equipped cars should not need any adjustment, as the lambda probe will automatically reset the mixture requirements to suit. Remember that cat cars will only accept a very mild cam change, as the ECU is set up to protect the converter. So, with road cars equipped with a cat, stick with just replacing the inlet cam with a standard 1800 16V original cam. This is cheap and easy, and gives the engine a far better response.

VR6 cams (12V models)

The VR6 has two cams, directly bearing onto the same cam followers as all the other hydraulic VWs. Removing and replacing the cams at home is quite a difficult job, fraught with many dangers.

The VR6 will respond to cams up to 260° on road-going cars. Rather like 16V Golfs, the VR6 benefits from replacing the cams last, after the cylinder head and exhaust system have been modified.

1.8T and 20V

Both of these versions of basically the same engine have limited potential for cam

A VR6 Schrick cam kit. It's all in there. *(Schrick)*

modification. Turbo cars can actually lose power with cam changes, as the increased forced induction pressure escapes through the exhaust valve with a performance cam.

Changing valvetrain components

Simply changing the cam on its own will not always work. There are many other components, subject to wear, that need to be replaced at the same time. The most important are the valve springs. Most of the road car cams, up to 285° duration, will work well with standard VW factory or equivalent parts. Beyond this point, the lift and duration will require special valve springs, and very careful checking of the ability of the valve spring to avoid valve spring crush (where the springs become 'coil bound' and there is not enough clearance in the spring to allow the valve to open fully). In this situation, it is essential to either fit special valve springs to suit the cam lift, or relieve the base of the spring seat to unload the spring, thus giving it more movement. If this is not done, the cam lobe will be quickly and expensively destroyed.

If you want to use a high quality high lift cam, buy a fully matched kit of components. Schrick race cams are available as a full kit with springs, retainers and top caps. Be very wary of unmatched components, as trail blazing is fraught with potential problems; let the manufacturers do the work for you.

The lighter the components that move up and down are, the less strong the valve spring needs to be, and the less strain there is on the parts that move at high speed. Fitting high quality alloy top caps to the valve springs will extend the rev range slightly, and lessen the chance of valve spring failure. VW valve springs last well, but the longer heavier valves in a 1600 GTI Mk1 can cause premature fatigue.

The springs cost very little to replace, but it is a job best done with the head off. However, there is a tool made to allow removal of the valve springs and seals with the head still in place.

Standard cam belts are fine at any state of tune, on all models. Replace 8V belts at about 60,000 miles and 16V belts at 50,000 miles.

20V and diesel belts are also 60,000 mile jobs. The VR6 does not have one! Be careful with the tension, don't over-tighten cam belts, they should be set so that you can twist the longest section through 90° with two fingers. Later cars have special tensioners that do the tensioning pressure internally.

On all models, especially at high mileages (say over 100,000 miles), replace the cam belt tensioner. They have sealed roller bearings that can suffer from old age, water ingress and over-tensioning. Failure of these is often the root cause of cam belt failures. If the tensioner seizes up, the cam belt lasts only seconds before breaking and destroying your valves. Rarely does this do more than mark the pistons, but it will require the removal of the cylinder head and fitting new valves.

The cam followers or lifters will rarely need replacing on solid shimmed cam engines, but hairline fractures can occur on the skirts of followers on very highly tuned race units. Full race cams can benefit from special lightweight Schrick cam followers, with the appropriate valve springs and retainers. Race cams tend to scoop the standard shims out of the small

The three cam belt tensioners. In order, left to right: 8V, 16V and 20V.

The 8V cam belt tensioner is narrower than a 16V.

retaining lip of the cam followers, especially at low revs. This is sudden and very destructive – the head and cam are wrecked in the process.

The secret is to fit the followers with a shim (called a lash cap) under the follower. The lash cap sits on the valve stem, and will need grinding to suit the correct valve clearance required by the cam. This is a tedious and long-winded procedure but well worth it for the added reliability it gives. I have never known one fail in a race car.

All hydraulic followers are prone to getting noisy, especially if the engine has suffered from infrequent oil changes. Noisy followers will rarely get better. The tiny holes that supply the oil to the hydraulic pump inside each follower will become blocked, preventing the pump from working. Sometimes, flushing the engine with special oil will work. Expect the followers to rattle for a few seconds initially, especially on cold days when the oil is thicker, but they should go quiet afterwards.

If you fit new hydraulic followers, try leaving them upside down in a container of engine oil for a day or two before fitting them to your engine. It allows the oil to prime the tiny pump in the follower, thus making the follower much quieter on initial start up. If they are not primed first, don't be surprised if the new followers sound like a major engine disaster on initial start up.

Cam verniers
Verniers can be a useful way of altering the characteristics of a cam in an engine. They

A Kent Cams 8V adjustable vernier with advance/retard marked.

replace the existing top cam belt pulley on an 8V, or the cam belt pulley and the chain sprocket wheels in a 16V engine. The basic theory is that advancing the cam timing relative to TDC will improve bottom-end power; conversely, retarding the cam will improve top-end power. The movement has to be very small, as contact between the valves and pistons must be avoided at all costs.

Taking the cam belt verniers first, always start by setting the adjustable vernier exactly as the original non-adjustable pulley, by putting it on top of the other and then marking the standard cam timing position. This avoids confusion when re-timing the cam, and it's less easy to bend the valves.

The rough and ready way to set the cam timing is to set the cam as originally set, then in small increments try altering the power range. This is best done on a rolling road. Remember, it will trade off top- and bottom-end power; you are unlikely to gain on both unless the cam is incorrectly made.

On a 16V, the vernier cam chain sprockets will require very careful setting up with a magnetic dial gauge used to measure the maximum lift, according to the cam manufacturer's specifications at TDC.

The correct method of setting the cam belt vernier is to first find TDC very accurately. This will require reaching into a cylinder with an extension on a dial gauge (actually not that easy!). When the engine is accurately on TDC, bend a piece of strong wire with a point ground at one end, and attach it to a suitable engine bolt near the lower crank pulley. Stick a 360° timing protractor to the crank pulley with Blu Tac, and bend the wire to point accurately to 0° (TDC). Be very careful not to move this setting or the protractor. Rotate the engine in its running direction until the wire pointer corresponds to the manufacturer's recommendation for the inlet valve degrees from TDC (this comes with a cam). Now set the inlet valve for maximum lift with the dial gauge by adjusting the vernier.

Now recheck it! It is surprising how far out the factory timing marks can be on the flywheel.

oil systems

The oil system is the life blood of your VW engine; neglect it at your peril. Modern oils are superb, with excellent lubricating properties even when the oil is cold, but a few minutes on small throttle openings pays huge dividends on a cold engine, as it gives the oil a chance to reach all the furthest flung parts of the system and get thinner as it warms up. Never use big throttle openings on a cold engine.

The job of the oil is obviously to lubricate the moving parts (effectively putting a film of oil between moving metallic components so they do not touch each other), but it also has to carry away the heat from these moving parts.

The oil needs on a standard Golf are not onerous at all, but a 1.8 Turbo driven flat out is a different matter. The system has to be able to cope with Granny's two-mile shopping trip and a track day in mid summer! Quite a difference.

Most modern oils of the correct grade seem to work well in our cars. We tend to use VW's own brand as it is superb quality and cheap to buy. It comes in three main types, standard multigrade, a semi synthetic and a full synthetic. The higher the grade the better the protection for your engine, and the longer it can last. Using a fully synthetic oil in an old engine is not usually cost effective, especially if it burns oil. Older high mileage engines are fairly slack internally anyway, so clearances are not so critical. It would generally be better to use a 20/50 or 10/40 oil in older engines.

Diesel engines usually need different oil, especially the latest generation of high output units. When the 115bhp PDI unit was introduced, we heard of several engines suffering piston failure after the first oil changes, because of normal non-specific oil being used instead of the correct grade.

The single most important way to protect your investment is to change the oil regularly, not necessarily simply based on mileage. We always change oil twice a year, regardless of the mileage. A high mileage motorway car will tend to be kind to oil – it's always fully up to ideal temperature, and does not suffer from stop/start town motoring. Granny's car (or a show car) can suffer badly from many runs at low engine temperatures, often in damp conditions, and a tiny yearly mileage. This engine will wear far faster when running than the motorway driven car, and maybe take four years to reach the normal oil change mileage. Simply changing the oil more often will help it considerably.

When you rebuild the engine, use a cheap multigrade oil to run-in your new engine. The oil will have to allow bedding in to take place, and as the engine should not be asked to work very hard or achieve high revs in the early stages, the oil quality is less important. Too high a quality oil will contain extra additives which stop this bedding in process. Never run-in an engine on synthetic oil. We suggest multigrade oil and 3,500rpm max until at least 500 miles. Then change oil and filter, still using multigrade oil, 4,500 max rpm until at least 1,500 miles. Then use a synthetic oil/new filter and occasional full throttle bursts (not held). After 3,000 miles, consider it run-in, although the engine will still be improving daily. VW units reach their best after 50,000 miles!

Always use a factory, or similar, oil filter. They are fitted with a non-return valve in the top of the filter to stop the oil draining back into the sump. This is easily spotted, so have a look to check if you use another make of filter. The factory filter is often made by Mann. All the filters are very cheap if bought at a GTI show, in a box of ten. Try to fill the filters partly before refitting as it then takes less time to fill up, thus giving a bit more protection to the crank shells.

A proper VW oil filter showing the essential non-return valve.

A magnetic particle trap that fits above the oil filter.

Magnetic filter traps

Magnetic filter traps are a good idea. They screw into the oil filter housing between the filter and the block to trap any foreign bits of metal before they can enter the engine. Clean them at the same time as changing the filter. There is not normally sufficient room to fit them if there's an oil cooler, as they go in the same space as the cooler thermostat!

Oil pumps

There are many variations, according to the engine type.

1100/1300 early cars pre-1986

These were the troublesome pumps and they regularly failed because of the design of the drive between the crank and the pump. The pump was a push-on fit onto a slightly curved drive flange on the crank. When the oil was thickest on a cold morning, the extra viscosity of the oil could cause the drive flange to destroy the crank drive, so the pump did not rotate, thus no oil pressure. This was very detrimental to the engine.

After 1986, the new hydraulic head engine needed more oil pressure to support the extra needs of the hydraulic tappets, and finally VW designed a decent reliable chain-driven pump, mounted in the sump. It is possible to fit this with lots of work to the early engine, but frankly never worth the labour! As the later head is a better design too, simply fit the whole unit.

8V and 16V oil pumps

All the oil pumps on 1500, 1600 and 1800 engines are very much the same design. They are driven by a gear on the layshaft.

An 8V's pump is driven by the slot in the base of the distributor, but a 16V's has a gear and different splined shaft. The pumps are the same but the shafts are different. They are all 30mm deep pumps with two equal size gears inside, and are very reliable in use. Dirty oil or lack of oil will quickly wear the pump. Luckily, they are easy to remove even with the engine in place.

There are several different design plastic baffles found on different age cars. They all clip onto the small gauze filter on the oil pump pick up. Expect to break off the plastic clips if you remove the baffle, as they will be very brittle from heat and age.

Removing the sump

Drain the oil from the engine and filter, then (using a ¼" drive socket set) remove the 10mm bolts at the flywheel end of the sump. These are difficult to get at, so start here! The rest of the sump bolts are much easier to remove. The oil pump is held by two long bolts, but always allow for the oil trapped above the pump that will run into your hair as you remove the pump!

To inspect the internals for contamination and wear, remove the small bolts and take the top off. Mark the gears so they can be refitted in the same relationship as before. Any roughness in rotating the drive shaft will mean replacing the whole pump. As the housing is alloy, any scoring from debris or dirt will lower the oil pressure, but it's easily checked.

When refitting either a new pump or the original, at least wet the gears with oil or grease to make it easier to get oil pressure after replacement. This is even more critical if it will be a long time before you intend to restart the engine. The lack of an internal seal can make getting pressure more difficult. There is no gasket between the block and oil pump.

After very carefully cleaning the gauze, refit making sure the oil pump drive correctly connects at the layshaft end. Replace the sump gasket and refit the sump and filter. The flywheel end bolts that were difficult to undo, are threaded into alloy so care is needed to avoid over-tightening or cross-threading the bolts.

Refill the sump, and spin the engine over with the plugs out. When the oil pressure comes up, the engine revs drop, as the extra load on the starter is felt. Refit the plugs and it's finished.

Priming 8V pumps

It's very easy to get oil pressure up on an 8V engine (not 1300) by removing the distributor and making a rod with a slotted end to fit the top of the oil pump shaft. It just pokes up through the base of the distributor hole. Fill the engine with oil and fit the filter. Use your electric drill, a battery one is best, and spin the shaft slowly until oil pressure is felt. The drill will twist in your hand as the extra load is felt. Spin for 30 seconds to prime the whole system so the first start-up is protected with instant oil pressure. Unfortunately, this is more difficult on a 16V as the drive is splined not slotted.

A common problem area

All models of the VW range, from 1300cc to 2-litre, suffer apparent loss of oil pressure. This is often blamed on oil pump failure, but rarely is. The fine gauze that stops any particles of dirt entering the oil pump can get covered with an almost invisible film of oil residue, making it difficult for the oil to pass through into the pump. This is more common than you may think; it is like a piece of cling film covering the gauze. Normally, only cars that have not had regular oil changes are affected, but cars that have stood unused (say waiting for sale) are likely to suffer this too. It is much worse when the oil is cold (thus thicker). Generally a good clean with carburettor cleaner will completely cure the problem. Follow the guide above for pump removal.

Uprating the 8V pump

The later the pump, the better the design. We use the standard 30mm 8V pump from a late 1800 for all 1600, 1800 and 1900 engines. The hydraulic tappet engines have excellent pressure and delivery in standard form. Retro-fitting this

pump to an early non-hydraulic car is an excellent idea. With no hydraulic tappets to feed, there is plenty of surplus pressure in hand.

The dreaded cause of many failures! An oil pump pick up gauze – this one is clean.

The three oil pump drives. Left to right: 30mm 1800, 36mm 2-litre and 16V 2-litre. Note the gear size and cut-out on the shaft for the crank clearance.

The 2-litre cars use a waisted drive shaft to clear No. 4 big-end.

Later 2-litre engines have a 36mm oil pump, but do not fit it to engines that are not fitted with oil squirters, or excess oil pressure will occur. You do not want very high pressure (not over 4 to 5bar max hot) but plenty of delivery is the secret of a sound long-lasting engine. High oil pressure can blow out seals or oil gallery plugs, and costs bhp to produce. I like to see about 3 to 4bar at a steady 3,500rpm on a hot engine.

Cold oil pressure will give ridiculous readings on some engines. Sometimes this very high oil pressure causes the problems mentioned. The only way that the pump can regulate the oil pressure is to open the oil pressure valve in the body of the pump and return the surplus to the sump. This means that the oil is not lubricating properly because it is still too thick. Try a thinner grade oil, as this will pass more easily into the oil galleries and give more prompt lubrication than the previous grade oil.

The pressure relief valve is pre-tensioned when the pump is made but can be removed with care for checking and adjustment.

Uprating the 16V pump

There is little difference in the 16V pump, as mentioned before, but oil pressure can be far lower than its 8V brother. There are twice as many hydraulic tappets to feed, and there is also a difference in the 16V block. All 16V

blocks have piston oil squirters fitted into the base of the oil gallery. The idea is to force a fine oil mist up onto the back of the pistons to cool and give extra lubrication when working hard. This system has good and bad points. The extra lubrication seems to make little difference even on thrashed cars. We have no more piston problems on 8Vs without the squirters than on 16Vs, however hard the engines are pushed. The oil pressure is lower because the squirters draw off the oil all the time, except at tickover or below 1bar pressure. Each squirter has a ball and spring set to close at less than 1bar, but in reality it's virtually impossible to check their operation.

They can be removed and the drillings blocked off with set screws. Large capacity engines will need this operation anyway because the oil squirters foul the pistons.

Later 16V 2-litre engines run a 36mm oil pump. This is a direct retro-fit to older engines with the correct length oil pick-up pipe. Obviously the pump has more capacity which can be useful, especially on cars with oil squirters fitted.

Sump design

The 1600 GTI and early 1800 GTI sumps had a sloping shape towards the centre and had a smaller oil capacity. As these cars had a proper oil cooler, this was no real problem, but later

Right: The oil squirter hole in a 'tall block'.

Far right: A 20V oil pump drive chain.

cars all have a flat base and more oil capacity, but no standard oil cooler. The sump can get very rusty and actually leak. The base is prone to knocks and can force the oil pick-up pipe against the inside of the sump, thus cutting off a good oil flow.

Beware of incorrectly shaped sumps, often in alloy. Many come from non-transverse-engined Audi models and none is really baffled correctly for a transverse-engined Golf. It's a shame they can't be used, as they look the business!

Uprating sumps and windage trays

Just occasionally, VW come up with a cheap good idea. The windage tray, found in all the later engines, is one. The crank moves a huge mass of oily air in a circular movement, especially at high revs. Not only does this create quite a bit of power loss, it also prevents the oil from dropping quickly back to the bottom of the sump, ready to be picked up again by the pump. The windage tray fits between the sump and the block, held by the same bolts as the sump pan. The surface of the windage tray is formed to prevent oil moving up and the slots in it suck the oil from the crank as it rotates. This reduces the chances of the oil frothing; the air mixed in with the oil can give poor lubrication at high revs, as the oil pump is not good at pumping oil and air.

Baffled sumps are a real necessity on fast road cars and track cars. I have seen many perfectly good engines wrecked in two laps on a track day, because of oil starvation. The oil can move up the sides of a standard sump really easily on a car with lots of grip and high G-forces.

The baffles stop the oil from rushing across the open space in the sump. Two simple baffles welded into the sump, with space allowed for the oil pick-up pipe, will suffice.

They must have holes or slots to allow the oil to get back to the centre, and not be so high that the crank hits as it rotates. Used with a windage tray, this will cure all the problems.

TSR sell the plates to fit yourself, or there are American complete metal sumps with built-in windage trays and flaps to control the movement of the oil. If you buy one of these

A windage tray.

A windage tray fitted on a block.

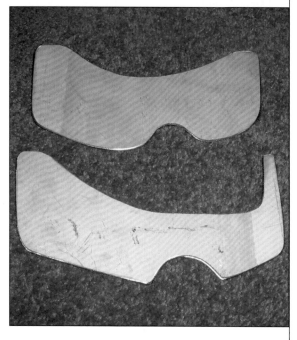

Oil sump baffles from TSR to weld into your own sump to make a DIY baffled sump.

A beautiful
Schrick alloy
sump and
fittings for
4-cylinder cars.
(Schrick)

sumps, take care to check that the little trap doors open the correct way, I had one with the doors fitted backwards! Sometimes the pins that hold the trapdoors are slightly bent or stiff. They may be sold from the States but they are made in Taiwan.

Schrick make a beautiful deeper alloy high-capacity sump that comes complete with longer bolts. This is the business if fitted along with a windage tray. The extra capacity helps with oil temperatures and gives a safety margin on hard-pressed cars too. Watch the extra depth does not put your sump in danger of contact with speed bumps if your car is very low.

Those of you with a VR6 or other Golfs will need to make them, as none is available off the shelf.

For race engines, there are dry sump applications. This system runs a pump to feed the oil into the engine and another to pump the used oil into a remote oil catch tank. This allows a very shallow sump to be fitted as the pumps are externally fitted. The oil capacity of the oil tank can be larger to keep oil temperatures lower, and give a greater reserve for long races. Dry sump systems are expensive and not really applicable to this book, but interesting nonetheless.

I realise that only a limited edition factory Mk2 and the four-wheel-drive Golf Rallye were released with the 160bhp supercharged engine, but this engine is a popular conversion for lesser cars.

The G60 unit is easiest to find in Corrados. Many thousands were produced, and as the Corrado was based on a Mk3 Golf chassis, fitting to other models is straightforward as long as the whole system and wiring is swapped over. Try to use the 02A cable gearbox as well, for the G60 engines are very torquey and destroy 020 boxes. The larger clutch is essential for reliability too.

The G60 unit may look similar to the normal non-supercharged 8V engine, but VW were at great pains to use very strong internals to suit the large extra power output. The block, crank, rods and pistons are all unique to the G60.

The cylinder head is basically a Digifant head with slightly larger ports and an extra mounting stud hole. They will interchange well.

There are actually two versions of the block. The four-wheel-drive Rallye version of the Golf was intended for motorsport, and has a slightly smaller capacity (code 1H and 1763cc) for homologation purposes to stay in the correct class. The Corrado, etc., has the more common unit (code PG at 1781cc).

Both units are otherwise the same. The compression is lowered to 8:1, with immensely strong pistons and huge 22mm pins. The rods are unique, but the bearings are normal 1800 Golf fitments. There are four oil squirters fitted for reliability. The oil pump is larger to supply the squirters and the oil fed supercharger. If you remove the supercharger, replace the oil line and check the oil feed is clear in the cylinder head as we have come across several blocked oil feeds. One customer had replaced two superchargers and both failed quite soon after fitting. The banjo union at the oil feed into the head had not been drilled at the factory!

The supercharger itself is mounted on purpose-made alloy brackets with the drive belt running via a tensioner from the crank pulley. An intercooler is also a standard fitment on both cars, but it is huge on a Rallye. It fits in front of the radiator for maximum cooling.

Unfortunately, they are very hard to find now, but it is an ideal design if you are having one made by a specialist.

The plumbing is obviously different if the big intercooler is fitted, as the bends are a different shape where the inlet pipe leaves the supercharger. The Rallye front intercooler fitting turns through 90° as it exits the supercharger.

The supercharger is a clever design but it has been given a totally unjustified bad name for reliability. The eccentrically mounted scroll is driven by a small toothed belt. This is the part that needs replacing every 60,000 miles or so, especially if the car has been unused for a while. It wears out or cracks through old age. If it breaks, the moving scroll contacts the fixed part of the scroll causing mechanical bedlam. The new units are hard to source and expensive, so always get an unknown supercharger rebuilt before it can break. Rebuild costs are low (compared to a breakage) from the specialists at Jabbasport.

The bearings and seals will also be replaced during the rebuild.

Take great care not to allow any foreign material in the air filter to fall into the air box during a filter change. The supercharger is like a Hoover when it sucks! Anything loose goes through it, causing premature wear or total disaster depending on the size of the object ingested. We had a customer who mislaid a nut during the rebuild, and used another. Guess where the nut was? On start up the brand new supercharger swallowed the errant nut, totally shattering the internals and causing much grief to the mechanic doing the job.

A rebuilt supercharger will last indefinitely; ours in the first G60 Mk1 in the UK was still going strong at 200,000 miles. We sold that engine to Australia, where it was fitted to a 1500 Golf 4-door. Most weekends it was used in this innocent combination to blow off V8 Holdens on the strip!

VW produced a small run of 16V G60 engines. These are as rare as hen's teeth and have no more power than a well-built 8V unit. The benefit of four valves per cylinder is nullified by the simple fact that an 8V breathes just as well with the gas under pressure from

A typical old G60 supercharger. Note the broken seal and alloy damage. This one is unrepairable and will need replacing with a new one.

The tiny toothed belt fits here on a G60.

the supercharger. The alloy supercharger mounts are complex and expensive, and the alternator needs remounting behind the engine. As an exercise in futility it is one of the best! Stick to the 8V.

Modifying the G60

The best value conversion on a G60 is simply to re-chip the ECU and fit a smaller pulley. This will come as a kit of parts and be a simple job. You will need to state the ECU box number when you are ordering the kit. This gives virtually 200bhp on a standard engine. A decent exhaust and manifold will help too. Use a big cone filter from Ramair, or similar, well shrouded from excess heat and with a good

A Jabbasport pulley and chip kit for a G60 to get 200bhp.

cold air supply. This is tricky in the crowded engine bay, but when driving on a warm day you will be glad you made the effort.

Get a large intercooler made if a Rallye unit is unavailable. Mount it *à la* Rallye in front of the radiator for maximum air flow. Remove the oil/water intercooler and find even more room for a proper oil cooler. It would be handy if the front panel was half a metre wider!

A big valve cylinder head is next. The lack of sodium filled exhaust valves does not seem to affect reliability at all. Do not fit a dump valve under any circumstances, as the excess air pressure recirculates into the inlet manifold ready for instant acceleration on the factory set-up, and that disappears if a dump valve is fitted. The supercharger is noisy enough without a dump valve!

The next step is a cam change. As the engine is not trying to suck its air, but is getting it under pressure, the cam change has little effect compared to a normally aspirated car. Schrick make a special G60 cam that gives good results on a well-modified engine. A normal sports cam will not work with this engine as the duration is too great. The supercharged engine will tend to blow the mixture straight out the exhaust valves in this case.

It is possible but difficult to build a 2-litre short engine for this engine. The normal 1800 block does not have strong enough rods (20mm pins) or enough space for low compression pistons. The later 2-litre 'tall block' is more promising, as the rods are 21mm and there is more space, but low compression pistons are not available and would need to be made by a specialist. We bought some from America, and they were useless, as the pins were under the oil control rings! Not ideal for good oil consumption!

All of these units would need a 2-litre crank and 82.5/83mm bore. The head gasket would overlap the bore or be weakened if the thin 2-litre gasket was used.

The 2-litre T4 van engine (also used on industrial engines) has a tall block with oil squirters and a long stroke 95.5mm crank, but an 81mm bore (as on a standard G60). This will accept the standard immensely reliable 1800 G60 head gasket with no modifications. The distance between the cylinder bores is also wider than on an 82.5mm 2-litre, also aiding head gasket reliability.

This long stroke unit will limit the rev range but, as the G60 only revs to just over 6,000rpm anyway, it's not an issue. After this, the gas in the inlet manifold goes supersonic and power suddenly drops off.

The rods have an enormous 24mm gudgeon pin, far larger than any other VW engine and ideal for the extra stresses of a supercharged (or turbo) unit. The extra weight of this big pin does not make itself felt at the revs it achieves. The standard low compression T4 pistons need decking by 2mm to get 8:1 compression for the supercharger to work best.

The crank is very tough, as it is virtually the same as a diesel crank. The pulley end drive is the same as a normal 1800/2-litre crank, so the cam belt is a normal 2-litre belt. When fitting

A T4 van rod and a G60 rod.

this to a G60, an alternator bracket needs fabricating because of the extra height of the block, and the normal covers and breathers, etc., need fitting from a T4 or 'tall block'.

This conversion will produce an amazing 240bhp with huge torque outputs. It is only limited by the pumping ability of the supercharger. It's superb in a Mk1 GTI.

Turbo conversions

The G60 or T4 short engine will also suit turbo conversions based on the 8V engine. Nothing from the later 1.8T unit will fit, as the engines are totally different. Using an exhaust manifold from a diesel leaves very little room for the inlet manifold, so aftermarket turbo kits use specially fabricated exhaust manifolds. There are still old Turbo Technics parts advertised in the magazines, and these work well.

The bottom line is simply that it is probably better, easier and ultimately cheaper to fit the excellent 1.8T unit as a turbo conversion, than play around with building a turbo engine yourself.

There are many American turbo kits available, some better than others, but watch the clearances of the turbo and exhaust around the RHD rack. Fitting any turbo unit will require electronic control to retard the ignition under boost, and increase fuelling at the same time.

The smaller 1.4 8V and 16V engines have an imported Italian turbo kit that works really well. It is very comprehensive, including an intercooler, all the plumbing and very neat turbo on an exhaust manifold – even a remapped ECU to improve the fuelling!

We fitted one to a Seat Arosa 1.4 16V and got over 160bhp! Amongst the smaller-engined cars, this engine (the same as in the equivalent Golf Mk3) is an ideal basis for achieving vast increases in output. The 8V cars also benefit from virtually the same kit but with different manifolds to suit the different porting in the heads. Installing the kit is a commonsense job, but it does call for a bit of fabrication to make things fit.

Normally the small-engined cat-equipped cars are difficult to tune because of the very limited cam choices, and these turbo kits are a useful way of producing over 105bhp from a 1.4 8V, and 140bhp from a 16V.

The kits can be adapted to fit virtually all of the many models using the same engines – Seats, Polos, etc. Fitting a base 1-litre car with a 1.4 is a straight swap; so many possibilities are opened up to the capable mechanic, and at little cost.

VR6 superchargers

Because the VR6 is quite an unrewarding engine to modify compared with the earlier 4-cylinder engines, another option is to supercharge the engine. As all VR6s were built after the legal requirement for retaining the cat came into force, the choice of cams is very limited. Supercharging will still allow the cat and the mild cams to work as normal, whilst increasing the volumetric efficiency dramatically.

A low pressure centrifugal supercharger (it looks and acts like a turbo but is driven by the crank) allows a boost of around half a bar to fill the cylinders very effectively. It is not too large, like most aftermarket superchargers, so suits the limited amount of space left in a VR6 engine bay.

It does not normally run an intercooler. It would benefit from one, though, but again space and plumbing limitations make it difficult. NSR supply a full kit including a rechip for the ECU. Up to 280bhp is possible, and it is easy to fit and remove.

There are American and German turbo kits on the market, but beware of space limitations on RHD cars around the steering rack area.

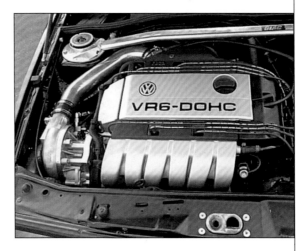

What a lovely sight. A VR6 fitted with an NSR supercharger kit.

diesels

The earlier 1600cc diesel engines in Mk1s were based on the existing 1500 petrol blocks. It was non-turbo and, while superbly economical, an unsuitable engine to modify. It was really a bit small for the cars, considering the diesel produced loads of torque but much less bhp than an equivalent petrol engine. VW didn't add a turbo until the Mk2 was introduced. As this car was heavier, the turbo was very necessary to get any real performance. Non-turbo cars were produced too!

This engine is fairly robust and very tuneable and it still suffers from being based on an existing petrol block. Diesel engines need very strong mechanical components to allow such high compression ratios (up to 23:1). The cranks and bearings give no trouble, but the pistons fatigue at very high mileages. The short engines are virtually the same on turbo and non-turbo and will happily interchange.

There is also a natural weakness from the siting of the head bolts, especially the corner bolts, as they are very close to the edge of the block. Over-tightening of these bolts, especially if any water or dirt was in the base of the threads, will cause cracks in the block. Always replace the stretch bolts on reassembly.

Cylinder heads also get major fatigue problems on these diesels. They crack badly between the valve seats, causing water/head gasket problems. Replace the head with a new one to cure this problem.

The 1600 diesel engines were the only VW unit we would not rebuild, as we found that reboring the already weak block caused movement inside the block and associated piston problems, especially if the engine was fitted to an overworked heavy car, or T2 camper.

Modifying the 1600 turbo diesel

The diesel responds well to head gas flowing, but retain the original standard valves for simplicity and because the exhaust valves are sodium filled for reliability. Clearances are very tight when the piston is at the top of the stroke, as the head on diesel units is flat, like the 1600 GTI, and the compression leaves a tiny combustion chamber.

When rebuilding the cylinder head, replace the valve guides as a matter of course. Take care to match the rather tortuous inlet manifold to the head, and check the exhaust manifold for cracks. I have seen several turbos wrecked from swallowing bits of cracked manifolds. Always retain the standard cam and cam timing.

The standard diesel injection pump is adjustable to suit the raising of the boost pressure, but it is either a trial and error or professional diesel specialist job depending on your skills.

If the head is removed at any stage, it is essential that the correct procedure for measuring the thickness of the head gasket required is rigorously followed, or the valves may touch the pistons (painful!), or if too thick a gasket is used, there is a lowering of the compression ratio and power will be lost.

To uprate the boost, modify the spring with a packing washer or similar. Increase the boost to no more than 1bar for the bravest! Any more and you will be picking up the engine parts in your driveway!

Fitting an intercooler from another model (Jettas had one as standard) is worth about 10% on any diesel, particularly if the boost is increased, as the squeezing of the air rapidly increases the inlet temperature. As the density of the air decreases with the temperature increase, efficiency falls rapidly. There is effectively less oxygen to support the combustion; far from ideal.

We modified a 1600 turbo diesel Mk2 a while back and easily achieved 100bhp from a 70bhp (SB coded) diesel. It flew, and still did the best part of 60mpg on a run abroad. That engine was still going strong at 200,000 miles.

Modifying 1900 non-turbo diesels

There are several different engines in this size, all with a decent non-petrol-based stronger block. Like the later petrol engines, it is taller by about 15mm, and can be fitted to 1600 cars as a whole engine or just the block. There are differences! The vacuum brake pump is a different diameter (use the later pump). If you use the 1900 cylinder head, note the inlet ports and manifold are a different shape.

The 1600 head is oval, but the 1900 head is D-shaped. The 1600 inlet manifold will not go straight onto the 1900 head without welding the ports to suit, but it is generally far easier to use a new 1600 head on the 1900 block.

The valves are ever so slightly smaller, but it is simple and the capacity increase is very effective anyway. You will also need the cam belt and covers from a 1900 to suit this conversion. You gain bhp, torque and the major advantage of a far stronger block.

The non-turbo car and T4 van engine will go well if the fuelling is increased and a sports filter added. This is useful if you have a heavy camper with the least powerful engine! About 15bhp increase can be expected.

VW produced an umwelt (clean) version of the turbo diesel. They added a tiny turbo to blow loads of clean fresh air into the engine to clean up the combustion, but there is little modification potential as the turbo is not really intended for power.

The later turbo diesel engines (from 1Z code onwards) are superb units to modify. The new stronger block allows huge power increases from the standard 90bhp with absolutely no mechanical strife. This engine is internally different from the earlier 1900 diesels, as the pistons and head are designed for the electronic injectors. It will not suit the earlier car as a replacement unit.

The management was electronic with an ECU to control it, and has electronic fuel injectors. The air movement is measured by an air mass meter with a hot wire as a sensor, whose temperature will vary according to the amount of air that is flowing over it. The signal will allow the corresponding fuelling to be controlled by the ECU. Each injector is controlled separately, unlike the earlier TDI unit which had a common fuel rail feeding all the injectors.

This unit will fit an earlier car but it is a major task. It will need all the engine wiring, ignition key and switch, ECU and complete dash internals including the instruments. The dash wiring can go into a Tupperware box under the seat, but it must be used to complete the immobiliser circuit, or it will only run for three seconds at a time! This allows all the original dash to be left in place.

A 1.9 diesel head has D-shaped inlet ports.

From bitter experience, it is essential to also use the diesel 02A gearbox. The older 1600 diesel 020 box will always quickly break and the clutch will slip as it is too small for a very torquey engine. Fitting the later 02A box is quite easy on a Mk2. TSR sell a kit of parts to mount the clutch cable and engine mounts. Only use a diesel spec gearbox, as the final drive is far higher to allow for the relatively low revs of a diesel unit.

Modifying 1900 turbo diesels

The simplest answer is to rechip the ECU. This is cost effective and easy to return to standard if you have warranty issues or want to resell the vehicle. Either send off the ECU to be rechipped or, far easier, buy an 'add on' unit. These simply plug into the wiring at the join in the loom. The unit intercepts the signals and tricks the existing ECU into refuelling the injectors. The 90bhp car produces 115bhp and lots more torque with one fitted, while the 110bhp engine makes a creditable 140bhp. You will find that the power also comes in earlier and fuel consumption is

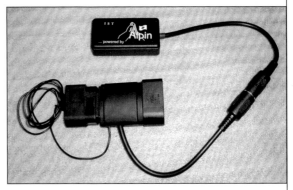

Diesel 'add on' uprate kits from Alpin.

slightly better. You can't afford to be without one of these units!

Adding a sports air filter or induction kit will aid power, but great care must be taken to ensure that there is no excess filter oil drawn into the hot wire air mass meter, or it will ruin the accuracy of the wire. As this unit gives problems enough of its own, extra care must be taken.

We worked with Allard a few years ago to produce a 170bhp 1.9TDI car. They built a huge intercooler to suit the car (a Mk3) and, with a flowed head and very much modified ECU, the car was staggeringly fast. When you consider that the maximum bhp and torque for a 2-litre 8V petrol engine is less, it makes you think how good a diesel is nowadays. It's all down to efficiency again.

PDI diesels

The new range of PDI diesels are direct injection into the cylinder. They come in lots of different bhp versions – 100, 115, 130 and 150bhp. Some are fitted with a superb 6-speed gearbox to make a very comfortable long distance car. These are my favourite VW engines.

All will rechip or suit 'add on' boosters. The 'add on' unit will cost more than the TDI units because the new PDI unit requires four separate 'add on' internals, as each direct injector is controlled separately. The 150bhp unit will give 180+bhp with 60mpg, and will easily see off a VR6!

All these engines MUST be run on the correct special oil to keep them intact.

Further mods include a larger intercooler, essential with big power increases, but space is limited, so visit a specialist like Allard for a really fine one-off build.

A very modified racing diesel 1.9 TDi, with over 220bhp and masses of torque.

engine swaps

Replacing existing engines with later or larger engines is a very cost-effective way to uprate a less sporty or basic vehicle. VW themselves are masters of 'parts bin engineering'. Remember, it requires quite a bit of mechanical knowledge. If in doubt, stick to a 1900/2-litre conversion. Also, bear in mind that engine swaps are only as good as the engine you source! A 150,000 mile G60 will be just about ready to give problems!

Mk1 and derivatives

The Mk1 and the other models based on the same chassis, were in production from 1974 to 1991, so there are still plenty to modify. It has also by far the lightest chassis, and predated the coming of the dreaded catalytic converter with all its limitations.

Its natural poise and superb handling make uprating the engine safe and brilliant fun. There was very little change in the mechanical details, even over such a long production run, so most problem areas were sorted by the end.

Several conversions are possible, but remember that starting any of these conversions from an 1100/1300 is more difficult; but only because more parts from a GTI will be needed to uprate the radiator, brakes, etc. The only chassis detail change will be the off-side engine mount. You will need to weld on a GTI mount (cut from a scrap car), as the mount on that side is different on a small-engined Golf. There will already be a preformed mark on the inner chassis rail against which to line up the mount.

Mk1 16V conversions

Probably the simplest and most effective conversion engine swap is the 1.8 16V from a Mk2 car. They are cheap and give 139bhp in standard spec. and this can be increased to 180bhp by modification.

The Mk2 has totally different engine mounts, so the Mk1 mounts and their carriers will need to be bolted onto the 16V lump. Replace the rubber mounts, preferably with uprated mounts to vastly improve the tautness of the conversion. There's nothing more horrible to drive than a new engine with old mounts.

You have the choice of gearboxes. The 16V gearbox is obviously ideal for the engine, but as there is very little difference in ratios, you can easily use an 8V GTI box. The carburettor box is wide ratio and does not suit the characteristics of the revvy 16V engine.

The 210mm clutches are interchangeable, but the clutch centre plate must be the correct one for the gearbox used, as the diameter of the centre shaft is larger on the 16V. To avoid clutch slip, the 16V will need at least a 16V standard or uprated pressure plate or diaphragm to clamp the centre plate correctly.

If you choose to fit the 16V box, remove the 16V gearchange linkage rods and links and rebush and refit the original Mk1 parts because they are different lengths. Rebushing is cheap and totally transforms the 'feel' of the gearbox. Remove the Mk2 100mm drive shaft output flanges from the 16V box and replace them with the 8V 90mm flanges. Take the opportunity to replace the flange oil seals at the same time. Remember to refill the gearbox with oil!

You can use the Caddy or later Scirocco (about 1989 onwards) 100mm driveshafts directly onto the 16V gearbox but NOT the Mk2 driveshafts (wrong length) or inner CVs. The inner CVs on a Mk2 have a different offset, and will disintegrate on a big bump.

Fit the 16V engine and gearbox into the engine bay carefully, making sure the engine is centrally mounted on the slotted end mounts. If it is hard up against one end, the CV joint at that end will bind and make grating noises.

The 8V radiator and plumbing will fit and work well with the more powerful unit, as long as it is not blocked internally. Never leave the radiator lying on its face for any length of time, as the core will get blocked with sediment. Sort out the top hose length. The Mk1 oil cooler housing fits a Mk2 16V engine (2-litre Mk3 is different) so it can be fitted if desired. Clean it very carefully, or replace it completely if the previous engine suffered a catastrophic disaster, or the debris from old blow-up will destroy your replacement engine too.

Now you need to fit the special 16V conversion exhaust manifold. The original cast

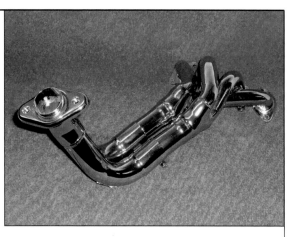

The useful 16V into a Mk1 Supersprint exhaust manifold.

unit is replaced by either an Ashley manifold or the superb chromed Supersprint manifold. The Ashley manifold is a tight fit, but adequate if you are on a limited budget. The Supersprint is the better fit, more expensive, and will also extend to suit the later taller 2-litre 16V engine. Your choice!

The Ashley manifold is a larger bore than the Supersprint, so an adaptor will need to be used to sleeve the manifold down to most aftermarket systems. In theory this is a bad idea, but in the real world it does not seem to show on the rolling road. Maybe the bore size is too large anyway?

The excellent Jetex system fits directly onto the Supersprint manifold, or if you want the quietest system, use the Supersprint, but it has rather a small bore for a modified engine.

The 16V uses an ECU to support the ignition. There are two options. First, simply unpick the standard wiring loom from the 16V donor car to remove the section of loom that joins the ECU to the coil and distributor, and reuse it. Second, buy just that section from TSR as a separate piece. You must fit the ECU to control the advance or retard, or you can, as a poorer but simpler method, fit an early Seat Ibiza 1.2/1.5 distributor from a pre-VW built car (1990 or so). This fits directly to the cylinder head and has mechanical advance/retard, but is not exactly correct for a 16V unit.

The injection is the preferred method of fuelling. Only resort to Webers if fuel consumption is less important or you started this conversion from a non-injection car. Fit the

16V metering head and sensor to a Mk1 GTI air box, and fabricate a bracket to allow the air box to sit on the off-side front chassis member. It fits quite naturally there, and all the braided pipes are the right lengths too.

The fuel line from the tank can either be carefully bent to come directly up the off-side, and new short lines and filter fitted, or like most people simply leave the original plumbing in place on the near-side and extend the fuel lines to the other side. There are already some suitable clips on the bulkhead to support the fuel lines away from the exhaust. Ideal! Always try to use steel or copper pipe, not very long rubber pipe. Always use 10bar flexible pipes to link the metal fuel pipes.

Fitting a later 2-litre 16V unit is exactly the same, but reuse the early k-jet system. It will cope well with the extra demands of the 2-litre, but you must fit the Supersprint exhaust manifold to allow for the extra height of the later block. Always swap over the mild 2-litre cams with the original 1800 16V cams to gain an extra 10bhp.

Another very effective swap is fitting the G60 supercharged Corrado unit into a Mk1. This gives 160bhp in standard form but up to 240bhp when fully modified.

The units are plentiful, especially in Europe, so go on the web if you have problems finding one here in the UK.

The engine can be fitted with the Mk1 engine mounts easily enough, but you should always try to keep the original 02A gearbox

One piece of a conversion kit to allow a cable clutch to be fitted to an 02A/02J later gearbox.

and linkage to this engine, for the extra strength. This requires fabricated engine mounts for the gearbox, and a cable clutch conversion (the original G60 is hydraulically operated). Raid the Seat parts bin for the parts, or contact TSR for a kit!

If you are short of money, the GTI 020 box fits well, but a Black Diamond or Sachs clutch will be very necessary because of the huge torque output of the G60 unit, especially if modified further. Expect a diff failure soon!

The G60 engine will not require a cat refitting, as the car is built before 1992, but the ECU and wiring will need to be reused. As the whole front loom is made as one piece, it can take a while to strip and sort the part you require. TSR will convert a front loom if you feel inadequate in this area. The ECU runs both the injection and the ignition on a G60.

Fit a good quality exhaust manifold from a normal 8V Mk1, and your choice in systems.

Fitting the intercooler is a problem. There are several ways you could try. We tried the standard unit where the battery had previously been, with a scoop in the bonnet and an alloy duct to ram the air through the intercooler. A purpose made front mounted intercooler is the best, but it is expensive.

Actually, putting the battery in the boot is an excellent idea on heavy-engined cars. It balances the car better, and leaves quite a bit more room in the engine bay for you to fill up again with the intercooler!

A cone air filter is the easiest to fit to finish the job off.

Our first G60 Mk1 was fitted with a straight-cut gear set (giving 60mph in first) and the excellent and very necessary Quaife LSD for strength and grip. In Holland at the GTI Treffen, it covered the whole timed strip in first gear, as, unlike our GTI International quarter mile drag, it had a chicane in the middle of the course. When the smoke cleared, the Germans were standing applauding! Great Britain–1, Germany–0.

The largest engine we ever fitted to a Mk1 was the VR6. It is a major exercise in rebuilding and fabricating (so not really an engine swap!), and it's heavy and clumsy for its output compared to a 1.8T engine!

To fit a 1.8T unit is also not for the faint hearted. It, too, will need an aftermarket (Motec or Emerald) ECU to run the engine because of the previously mentioned problems with the immobiliser systems.

The actual engine fits, but entails drilling engine mounting bolt holes in the block or reusing other holes and making the mounts to suit. The exhaust downpipe will need making from scratch in stainless steel for long life. There are many specialists offering this service in the magazines.

It must use the original 02J box and clutch because of its power and torque. Only 1.8T units from longitudinally fitted installations will suit this conversion, as Passat and Audi units are quite different. Seat Ibiza/Leon units are ideal. It is quite possible to achieve 250bhp or more (with your fingers crossed) from this engine … pretty impressive in a light Mk1.

Mk2 cars

You would not normally bother to convert an 8V Golf Mk2 to 16V, as it's available anyway, but the G60 is superb in a Mk2 two-wheel drive chassis. We have converted many cars; they were all huge fun and very quick. The best

one was an innocent grey four-door, fitted with a TSR 2-litre unit (240bhp) and six-speed Quaife gearbox with limited slip differential. A real 'sleeper' if ever I saw one.

The fitting is easier than a Mk1, as the engine mounts are the same on a Corrado as a Mk2, with the exception of the front mount. Either fit a stronger Vibra-Technics front mount (virtually impossible if the engine is already in place), or use the Corrado cross member with the inset mount. The wiring and ECU are required as on the Mk1, but the exhaust is made easier by using a standard 8V manifold and downpipe or TSR exhaust manifold.

Another look at the 20V Mk2.

A 16V system is exactly the same as an 8V system but for its larger bore, so ideal for this conversion. Use the 02A gearbox and TSR fitting kit for simplicity and reliability.

The VR6 will fit into a Mk2 and give loads of power and a very pleasant engine note unique to a 6-cylinder. Source either a 2.8 Golf (but not Sharan as it's only 140bhp!) or 2.9 Corrado unit with all the wiring and cooling parts. Virtually everything will need swapping over, including the cross member and radiator/fans, etc. Again TSR will sort the wiring for you if it's a worry! Fit the whole unit, but remember to change over the wishbones/anti roll bars and rack for the Mk2 examples, as the Corrado/

Golf 3 is wider, and the rear track will end up narrower than the front if you forget! Fit poly bushes at the same time!

The VR6 has a power steering pump, so it's an ideal time to fit power steering to your Mk2 if it was not there initially. You will need it with a huge VR6 'lump' dangling in the engine bay!

The VR6 runs twin fans and special relays. You can run the VR6 on a turbo diesel radiator, but be careful to find a rad with the different positioned outlets to suit the engine. The drive shafts fit with no problems.

The 1.8T follows the Mk1 guide but, again, the engine mounts are easier to fit. This is the ultimate unit in a Mk2 car for tuneability and strength.

A purpose-made intercooler is best across the radiator. Follow the guide for fitting the 02A/J gearbox, as before.

Mk3 cars

It gets easier, but remember these cars need to retain the cats at all times. The track is correct anyway, the same as a G60 Corrado or 1.8T, so the suspension will fit. Only the 1.8T will really suit this car, but it is fun! We built a 1.4 single point car into a 250+bhp turbo car a few years ago. The car had been a 'one family' car, owned by mum before passing it on to her son. I wonder if she would still go out in it.

That's better, another 1.8T has found a new home in a Mk2.

engine mounts

The engine has to be supported by flexible rubber mounts to avoid harshness and vibration when the car is driven. Transversely mounted engines, like all the Golf family, tend to twist forwards and backwards under acceleration and braking. On a Mk1, this movement gives the exhaust downpipe a hard time and tends to twist gear linkage out of line. There are four engine mounts, one at either end on the engine/gearbox unit, and one at the front and one at the rear of the engine. All bolt directly to the car body.

The pulley end mount is best changed whenever the engine is out, as it is quite difficult to remove in place. The centre of the rubber is slotted to allow movement, but often can collapse completely allowing the engine to drop down. The thin Allen key headed bolts are usually rusty and stubborn, and the big bolt through the centre of the mount can rust solid. This will require cutting with a hacksaw blade to remove. A good dose of WD40 weeks before removal may help. The new mount will need to be pressed into the circular housing before refitting.

The gearbox end mount is rarely in poor shape as it only suffers old age and not oil contamination. It is like the pulley end in design, but smaller and easy to replace.

The front and rear mounts are also easy to replace and make a huge difference to engine movement.

The front rubber cushion is replaced by a poly mount; the rear is available in poly or rubber. We have found the poly mount to be harsh and unreliable and the captive bolts tend to pull out in hard use. Use a diesel rear mount as it's made of a harder rubber.

The two large rubber Mk1 end-engine mounts, the larger is the pulley end mount, and the smaller is the gearbox end mount.

Mk1 pulley end mount and bracket ready to be pushed in.

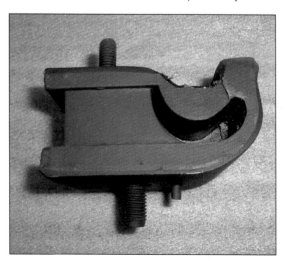

Far left: The diesel Mk1 rear mount.

Left: A standard Mk1 front mount and its poly replacement.

Mk2 rear engine mounts from Vibra-Technics with the two alternative mounts.

Left to right: Vibra-Technics front mount Mk3, rear Mk2/3 and front mounts.

Mk2 engine mounts are completely different from the Mk1 mounts, as the engine is supported on a sub frame. There are three mounts only, two at the rear and one at the front. The rear on the engine comes in two totally different shapes, with three bolts on top or one big bolt. The gearbox rear mount is easy

The most essential Mk2 Vibratec mount at home.

to change, but the front mount is usually in a worse condition.

This mount bolts onto the front cross member and has to support all the weight and twisting movement of the engine. Early 1984 cars had a better system, but it is no longer available, unfortunately.

All the rest, including 16Vs, have a fluid-filled rubber mount that usually has collapsed from loss of fluid. If your engine jumps up and down, replace this mount first with an excellent Vibra-Technics front mount. These front mounts are available in road form and a harder competition form, and feature an alloy housing with replaceable rubber centre. Using these mounts will make excessive engine movement a thing of the past, especially on a powerful car. They are easy to change (except on a G60 because of lack of space, but it will fit if you struggle!).

Vibra-Technics mounts are available for all the Mk2 and Mk3 cars, including the VR6. The Mk3 cars have a different front mount set down into the cross member, but it works in the same way. Some Seats and Skodas use similar mounts too.

Mk4 cars are well supported by standard mounts, but the 'push pull' mount under the engine can be improved by fitting a harder bush, available from the States.

For rally cars only, VW motorsport make a virtually solid kit! It needs to be welded on.

rolling roads

A small section explaining the good and bad points of rolling roads may be of interest.

When I first started TSR Performance, nearly 20 years ago, there were very few rolling roads available to the general public. Most tuning was done by experts with a feel for the machinery, and road tests to test the end-results of the tuning were common. Traffic was much less dense, there were few speed limits and the police only had Morris 1000s. The cars, too, were considerably less complicated, had no electronics to confuse the issue, and emissions were not tested.

Our rolling road came out of the MG factory at Abingdon, and had been used to set up the 'works' Minis and Healey 3000s a few years before. A rolling road with a history!

The principle used to measure the bhp is quite simple in theory. Two heavy rollers support the driven wheels, and they drive an electronic generator (actually a Telma lorry brake on the Sun unit we use). This, in fact, measures the torque produced, but plotted against road speed will give the bhp figures. Most figures are taken in fourth gear.

It makes a big difference if a lower gear is selected as it alters the torque considerably. A lower-geared GTI will give about 10bhp more than a wide ratio carburettor car in fourth gear, even if they have the same engine power outputs.

Beware of rolling road operators who insist on using a lower gear as this will give unrealistic outputs!

A rolling road allows tuning under full power conditions and under load, as well as being monitored by diagnostic tuning equipment during the testing. This is very much more accurate than simply revving up the engine off load.

On a Golf, normally reckon on losing about 25bhp or so to the transmission after the flywheel, as wheel bearings, brake pads and driveshafts all sap the available power, and require engine power to drive them.

When tuning a car, do not simply add up the 4bhp gain from the air filter, the 30bhp from the cylinder head, 12bhp from the cam, etc., and expect this to be the actual figure obtained. The actual figure is inevitably lower as, while each part contributes to the efficiency of your engine, the overall bhp is a combination of the figures not a sum of the figures.

A totally standard 1800 GTI makes about 90bhp at the wheels, a 16V around 120bhp at the wheels, and a VR6 about 150bhp. Turbo cars can be disappointing on the rollers as the intercoolers do not get much cooling air on the rolling road. The cooling fan is like a hairdryer compared to the forced draught of 80mph on the road.

The petrol used needs to be considered too, if good figures are needed to impress the

The rolling road.

crowd at a 'shoot out' day. All modern cars running a catalytic converter will automatically retard the ignition if the engine 'pinks', and this costs power. A VR6 can lose 20bhp right at the top end on a hot day if the engine knock sensor detects 'pinking'. The smooth power curve will suddenly show a drop followed by gradual increases of ignition advance and power until the 'pinking' is detected once more. Use Shell Optimax or BP Ultimate during power runs and track days. At the time of writing, these have the best octane rating and there is less 'pinking' potential.

The atmospheric pressure and humidity on the day make a difference too. A cold wet day is best for the figures, but can make getting some grip on the rollers a bit more difficult.

Tyre and wheel sizes also affect the figures; to compare different cars on different tyre combinations is dangerous. The width of a tyre affects the footprint of that tyre, and the greater the footprint the more friction it creates, thus the less power you will see. Also, the diameters can affect the gearing, as mentioned before.

Never put a road car with a new engine on a rolling road until at least 1,000 miles have been covered to allow for some running in. Race and competition units need a sensible approach in this area. Giving a newly-rebuilt engine serious gyp straight after building is seriously dodgy and can damage the unit and dent your pocket severely.

Finally, remember that the end-result of your rolling road tune depends on the skill of the operator.

Carburettors were used on all VW models except GTIs until the introduction of catalytic converters, which saw the fitting of injection systems. All 1100, 1300, 1500, 1600 and 1800 Golfs have various different versions of the rather fickle Pierburg carburettor.

Carburettors and fuel systems

As an everyday carburettor, the Pierburg was fine when it was working as it was intended to do, but it has serious limitations when old and tired. The carburettor was complex and prone to many faults with the sensors and drives attached to give it tick-over control; it is totally unsuitable for a modified engine.

The venturi, or hole in the centre of a carburettor, through which all the air passes is known as the choke. (This has nothing whatever to do with the choke that enriches the mixture for starting. It can be confusing!)

Some of the very basic engines used a single venturi (choke) carburettor, but the later cars always use a progressive twin-choke. Often it was far from progressive in use! The twin-choke carburettor only opens the smaller primary butterfly at light throttle, but under large throttle openings, it opens the larger secondary butterfly as well, thus flowing a great deal more fuel/air mixture.

If your Pierburg is showing signs of being poorly, with erratic tick-over and uneven running, then do not waste time and money repairing it, but save up and fit the excellent replacement Weber to suit your application. As before, the majority were twin-choke to suit the original inlet manifold.

There are numerous versions available, but even though they are simply intended as replacement carburettors for the Pierburg set-up previously fitted, they have great potential for extra power and, most important, they are simple in operation and easy to keep in tune.

All the replacement Webers come with all the fittings needed to convert the car. These generally include the new base plate, studs and air filter adaptor, so the original air filter housing can be reused. When fitted, the replacement Weber looks much like the original. Insurance companies regard the Weber as a substitution for the original so no extra premium is asked.

All Webers have manual choke operation, so a choke cable is supplied. This is really a blessing, as it's one more way of simplifying things. Automatic chokes are always an unreliable area on an older car. What is always a surprise is the pile of parts left over when the Pierburg is replaced by a Weber! None of the vacuum and electrical connections is reused. Carburettor replacement such as this should always be the first thing you do if you intend to run a modified carburettor Golf of any type.

The fuelling can be easily reset for a modified engine, as all the jets and venturi can be uprated cheaply, the parts being readily available from many specialists, but it is virtually impossible to reset the carburettor on a modified engine without the use of a rolling road.

All the original carburettors, and replacement twin-choke Webers, sit on a rubber flange that bolts between the inlet manifold and the base of the carburettor. These flanges come in a number of variants, so be sure if you buy a new one to replace the leaking old one. It's easy to tell if it's developed a small leak. Simply move

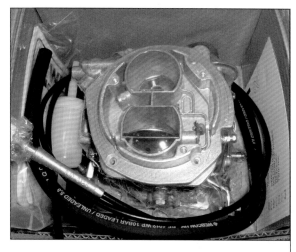

Opposite: A 1300 Weber twin-choke replacement carburettor kit fitted.

Left: A Weber replacement carburettor. There's lots in the box for the conversion.

the carburettor around with the engine running. If the revs alter, it is probably due for replacement. Always replace the rubber flange if you fit a new carburettor.

Replace the air filter with a performance filter at the time of fitting a new carburettor, but do not fit a replacement sport filter unless you wish to suffer carburettor icing on colder days. It's common to have this problem even on days well above freezing, but when the air is humid or foggy. That's the reason for the warm air pipe leading from the exhaust manifold to the air filter.

The breather from the rocker box leads into the air filter. By law the engine is expected to ingest its own breather oil fumes, but in reality it can cause serious problems. The bigger capacity carburettor engines tend to suck the oil from the rocker box breather under large

Just two examples of the many rubber flanges fitted on carburettor Golf engines. Take care when ordering a new one!

throttle openings, caused by the inadequate volume of air that the standard air filter can flow. It is best to add a small breather filter to this instead of letting it get sucked back into the air box. Alternatively, use a remote air box of bigger dimensions. A Rover Montego unit is ideal and cheap to source.

All the standard carburettor fuel pumps are adequate even in quite high stages of tune, but the 1100/1300 pumps are very prone to leaking at the flange, and must be replaced if this is the case.

Many of the later cars run a flow and return system to the tank, and a swirl pot on the front of the cylinder head, to avoid flooding or starvation. Both systems are OK for performance applications.

There are several high-performance electric fuel pumps available, probably the most common being those from Facet. They come in various capacities to suit your conversion. The solid state series of pump comes in three versions: 'road', 'fast road' and 'competition'. All must have a good quality fuel filter fitted between the tank and the pump to stop any dirt or water jamming the valve in the pump. The alternative transistorised interrupter pumps are less prone to stoppages. The Silver (18 galls/hr) and the competition Red (40 galls/hr) are excellent units. Obviously you need to fabricate a blanking plate to cover the original fuel pump hole if running an electric pump.

The alternative electric high-performance fuel pumps (Facet, etc.) must be fitted with a pressure regulator to stop the pulsing of the electric pump causing the needle valve in the carburettor from sympathetically pulsing and raising the float chamber level, thus flooding the engine. The regulators are available in several different forms – all are adjustable for pressure, and some have alloy or glass traps – the choice is yours. Always mount the electric fuel pump BELOW the height of the carburettor, again to avoid flooding. Obviously route fuel lines well away from exhausts and heat sources. Use steel pipe where possible or the correct good quality fuel line where steel pipe is impossible. Also, use proper fuel line clips to locate the pipes, not Jubilee clips, as they can squash the rubber pipe.

Fuel tanks

The tank is different on a GTI from a standard carburettor car. Fuel surge is to be expected if you run a Mk1 tank much below half full in competition, as the fuel can move up to one end allowing the pick up pipe to suck air not petrol. The answer is obvious.

The Mk1s suffered from problems, too, with the metal tank, but later Mk2s onwards have plastic tanks.

The Mk1 tank will rust, especially if the car is stored for a long time without much petrol in the tank. The air forms a fine rust film inside the exposed tank. This falls to the bottom of the tank the first time the tank is filled with fuel, and causes mayhem in a carburettor or the injection system. The cure is to keep a stored car full of petrol; it may even go up in value while it sits there!

Also, the Mk1 suffers from a very rust prone petrol filler neck. This is metal and runs through the rear wheel arch between the filler cap and the tank. Most cars will have had problems with the neck rusting through, again causing water from the rear wheel spray entering the fuel system, and rust getting into the tank. Both are expensive to repair. The actual filler neck is cheap and readily available, so remove yours and check it carefully. A really good coat of Waxoyl or Hammerite will greatly increase its ability to stave off rust. Sciroccos and Cabrios have similar but slightly different filler necks with the same problems.

If you think you are suffering from rust in the tank, make sure there is no source of sparks/naked flames, etc., tip up the rear seat, roll back the flooring, and remove the large circular plate in the rear floor above the fuel tank. Underneath you will find the fuel gauge wiring and the top of the fuel sender unit. Unscrew it and gently and carefully remove it. It is best done with a low fuel level and in a well ventilated area for safety and fume reasons. Look into the tank, and rust or water will be easily seen. Rust is easiest to remove, using an extendable magnet, but you need to find the source to cure it.

Water is more serious, as it does not compress, and will not pass through the metering head slots. Try using a big syringe and go fishing for the water, as it is quite separate from the petrol. Try an additive for the fuel system (Wynns, etc.), as this will break down the water into smaller molecules.

Alternative carburation

So far we have simply talked about replacement carburettors, but there comes a time when larger carburettors are required. For outputs of over 120bhp, a pair of side-draft Webers will be needed. For Weber, also read Dellorto, they are very similar in design but less readily available.

There are three sizes of carburettor available, but really 40mm or 45mm will be plenty big enough. There is a 48mm Weber, too, but it is too large for our engines. Avoid the old Webers with no air hole into the float chamber, as fitted to many production cars in the 1970s.

The Weber DCOE series can be re-choked and re-jetted to suit every application possible, and can give a massive power boost to a carburettor engine, but at a cost in fuel consumption. As each choke of the Weber has an individual fuel pump jet, every time you squeeze the accelerator, a jet of fuel squirts into the carburettor to give excellent initial response. Town driving can result in fairly frightening fuel consumption. In cruise, the carburettors are far more fuel efficient, but noisy.

To fit 2 x DCOEs you will require:
1. A pair of new or recon Webers, either 40 or 45 DCOE.
2. A proper quality throttle linkage kit, usually top fitting linkage with a single cable.
3. An inlet manifold to suit the cylinder head application used, i.e. 8V or 16V.
4. A pair of suitable air filters, as deep as possible considering the room available.
5. An uprated fuel pump as mentioned before.
6. 'O' ring set and gaskets for inlet manifold.

There are several points to be aware of before buying the gear! First, watch the clearances as some of the cars are an extremely tight fit. This will dictate the depth of the ram pipes and air filters. You must run ram pipes inside the filters for proper pick up.

The often used manifold for an 8V Weber conversion.

A late model 1400 Polo or Golf manifold to allow the fitting of twin Weber DCOEs. The ports are different from an early 1300 car.

A 1300 early hydraulic unit fitted with 2 x Weber DCOEs in a Polo. Note the socks as an alternative to filters.

Here are some tips for when fitting Webers to the different engines:

1100/1300 Mk1 – Only consider it if the later 1300 hydraulic engine has been fitted, then its brilliant! We achieved 110bhp from a well modified 1300. Locating an inlet manifold can be tricky now as it's older. There are several different types according to age/head type. There is plenty of room for the Webers as the engine leans forward.

1300 Mk2 – Exactly as above, except any car post-1986 will already have the later hydraulic engine.

For cars fitted with later Polo engines, say 1400 or 1600 Polo 8V units in an earlier car without the legal requirement of a cat, a different inlet manifold is required, but it's a superb conversion. Try a 1400 16V Polo engine in an older Polo with Webers!

For 16V Golf engines, either in a Mk1 conversion or a Mk2 16V with the injection removed, it's easy with the correct inlet manifold. There's a reasonable amount of space as the carburettors face forward, so make sure

the filters or filter socks are clean and not holed, as it's really easy for the carburettors to swallow a stone.

8V 1500, 1600 and 1800 engines – This is the difficult one to get right. The engine leans back towards the bulkhead, making clearance tight, and the available space is reduced further by the clutch cable which runs in the same area. But, with care, it is certainly possible.

The Weber inlet manifolds often need a bit of fettling to get the ports to match up correctly if cheaper manifolds are used. There are two types of 'O' rings available to seal between the inlet manifold and the Webers. For simplicity use the latest single 'O' ring already glued in a carrier. The older multi-part type with separate plastic or alloy carriers are difficult to fit. There are too many bits to drop down the back of the engine, never to be seen again. Also, again for reliability and simplicity, use the modern rubber tensioning system, rather than the older Thackery washers.

You will find it best to part build up the Webers on the bench before attempting to fit the whole assembly on to the engine.

The original Allen key studs that retained the original inlet manifold will no longer fit, except in the outer holes, so buy some studding of the same thread. Measure the depth you require and cut the studding. When you have tried the inlet manifold on the studs, make sure you can get nuts on the end of each stud. Remove the studding and Loctite the studding in to the cylinder head, so that in future the stud will not unscrew if you remove the nuts. Never use locknuts as they tend to unscrew the studding when they are being removed.

Fit the Webers carefully onto the inlet

A 1.4 16V Weber manifold from Germany.

manifold and leave the air filters and bell mouths off at this point. Be very careful that the carburettors are correctly tensioned equally at the rubber tensioners. Sort out the throttle linkage you have bought, making sure full throttle is obtainable and nothing is sticking open, as this certainly adds to the excitement.

Fit a new inlet manifold gasket and then slide the carburettor/manifold assembly onto the studding you have fitted to the cylinder head. Add the nuts and the two Allen key bolts. Fit the bell mouths and filters. As space is very tight you may find it easier to make or buy a filter box and add a remote air filter. Very short bell mouths are available for restricted space situations. Webers run poorly without bell mouths, as the air flow at certain revs is dramatically affected by sudden changes in direction. Air filter socks can be substituted for air filters to make things fit the limited space, but they need to be attached to the bell mouths carefully, and they tend to have a short lifespan, mainly because they rub against the bulkhead and cables.

Carefully run new fuel lines well away from the exhaust. Problems often occur when the car has been used hard, especially in competition, as the heat from the exhaust manifold will spread upwards into the Webers, causing petrol to expand and run down the exhaust manifold. This is dangerous and an accident waiting to happen! Try to shield the exhaust from the carburettors so the heat can't build up, or add a small fan to blow cool air around the carburettors/exhaust manifold area. I fitted an on-off switch to my fuel pump so I could switch it off just before I stopped at the end of a hill climb, to lower the level in the float chambers and allow for a bit of expansion.

If these Webers are being fitted to a car that previously had an injection system, there are a few points to be aware of:

1. The injection fuel pumps run at over 2.5bar, (40–75lb psi) depending on the car. As carburettor cars need a maximum of 4lb psi, there's no way the injection pump can be regulated to that low pressure. By-pass the original pump and accumulator and fit the proper Facet type of pump. The new pump is best fitted in the engine bay.
2. The holes in the cylinder head in the injection engine will need blocking off. There are several different approaches. On an 8V GTI previously running on K-Jet, use gearbox oil level plugs; they screw directly in. A later Digifant car has small diameter holes, so machine up four plugs to suit. Do not simply epoxy the hole, as I have seen several blow out when the engine backfired.
3. The original fuel filter is reusable along with the main fuel lines. With the injection removed there is plenty of extra space created for the fuel pump, etc.
4. Do not 'piggy back' the electric fuel pump electricity feed from the coil, or a weaker spark will be produced. Either run a new fused (ignition on only) feed from the fuse box or reuse the existing relayed original pump feed.

The ultimate in fitting 2 x Webers is to fit throttle bodies with an ECU to control the system, including installing a lambda probe to supply information to the ECU. This is the only way to stay lawful on a cat-equipped car. The throttle bodies have throttle position switches and, according to the system and its complexity, other sensors like air temperature, throttle pot, etc. Most kits come with the wiring included.

The ECU generally comes unmapped, so it takes a good day at least on the rolling road to set it up. After all, it takes the manufacturer many millions of Euros to program an ECU!

To look at, the throttle bodies are essentially similar to Webers, containing the butterflies and electrical fuel injectors. They fit on the standard Weber inlet manifolds, and are completely suitable to very high outputs yet retain the cat in working condition – and will suit a modern car with an MoT. Many also support a purpose-built ignition system using a lot of the same sensors.

A 2-litre crossflow with a big valve head and race cam made over 186bhp at the wheels (220 or so bhp). The amazing torque and total drivability was outstanding, even running a 304° cam. It ticked over at 800rpm, and was not cammy at all.

It's simply the only way to get ultimate power!

injection systems

The first application of an injection system was with the introduction of the Mk1 GTI 1600 in the late 1970s. There was an immediate improvement of fuel metering over the previous carburettor fuelling systems. The Bosch K-Jetronic system was very accurate and fuel efficient but entirely mechanical, with no electronic control, unlike later Digifant Mk2s.

K-Jetronic injection

K-Jet is the simplest injection system. On a Mk1 it used a gravity-fed fuel pump, fitted beside the tank, to feed petrol at 5bar pressure via an accumulator (to keep the fuel pressure up for

A K-Jet metering head.

A K-Jet warm-up regulator; this one has the extra vacuum pipe fitted to allow extra fuel under hard acceleration.

starting) and a large fuel filter to the metering head. The metering head distributed the fuel by high pressure pipes to the injectors.

The fuel pressure was controlled by a warm-up regulator fitted on the front of the engine block, and linked to the metering head by braided fuel lines. These lines have different sized ends so they can't be fitted incorrectly. The regulator has some control over the fuel pressure, for adding extra fuel until fully warmed up.

Under the metering head is, effectively, a see-saw arrangement with a circular plate in the air flow that gets lifted by the vacuum of the engine when the throttle is opened. At the other end of the see-saw is the fuel metering pin under the metering head. As this drops, it allows more fuel to enter the system to exactly balance the added air flow. Once it is set this system is very accurate and robust. Unused fuel returns to the fuel tank by another fuel line. The fuel pump has a built in non-return valve.

The throttle cable acts on a twin-choke throttle body bolted to the inlet manifold. This is supplied with air only from the big black plastic tube from the air flap and filter. The fuel injectors fit directly into the head.

Cold starting is helped by a fifth injector set in the end of the inlet manifold. It is controlled by the thermo time switch in the top hose fitting on the head. It is simply a temperature switch. To increase the tick-over during the warm-up period, a rotary air bleed valve is fitted on the rear of the inlet manifold.

Fuel lines Mk1/Cabrio Scirocco

The steel fuel lines are very prone to rust on these older cars. The factory fuel lines were supplied in pre-bent form, and were very awkward to fit to the car. The lines run behind the steering rack, necessitating removal of the rack. The car needed to be raised well off the ground on a ramp, preferably a two-pillar type, to get sufficient room to feed the new pipes through the hole in the chassis leg. As if this wasn't bad enough, the factory fuel lines have been discontinued. The Mk2 uses very high pressure plastic lines, but the ends are different, and these can be adapted to suit the Mk1, or you can get your local hydraulic (maybe tractor) dealer to make the correct ends on a steel pipe. The fittings are standard metric fittings.

Fuel lift pump – Mk2 models

Later Mk2 cars (pre-Digifant) had the extra benefit of a small extra fuel pump fitted inside the tank to lift fuel into the fuel pump.

Mk1 cars always suffered from fuel starvation if the tank was low on fuel. At the same time that this pump was introduced on Mk2 Golfs, many other models based on the Mk1 were also fitted with it – Cabrios and Sciroccos, for instance. This pump often gives problems on all these cars, and if your car runs better with a full tank, it's a likely suspect. You can remove it by taking the cover from the fuel tank sensor and withdrawing the whole sensor with the pump attached. It's a good opportunity to check inside the tank for contamination; water shows as droplets, and any rust can easily be removed with a small pen magnet.

Tuning K-Jet systems

To tune a K-Jet car, the fuel pressure must be set first. There are shims inside the pressure relief valve on the side of the metering head to adjust this. The correct pressure gauge and fittings are needed. The information is in the relevant Haynes Service and Repair Manual.

With the pressure correctly set, use a gas analyser to set the mixture. Generally, the engines like about 1.5/2 CO. To adjust the mixture, use a long 3mm Allen key through the hole (sometimes blocked off) between the metering head and the air flap. It simply screws clockwise to enrich the mixture, and anticlockwise to weaken. Always adjust from weak to rich on a fully warmed-up engine (or the cold start enrichment system will still be operating).

NEVER rev up the engine with the Allen key in the adjuster, always remove it after each adjustment. It adjusts by moving the fulcrum of the see-saw, and will jam if the tool is left in. Very little movement makes quite a difference in the mixture CO.

If the car runs well when hot but badly when cold, suspect the warm-up regulator, as they are prone to problems with dirt and rust.

A lift pump found inside the fuel tank on most GTIs other than Mk1s.

Take care that rust or water does not enter the system from a rusty filler neck, as water will not pass through the tiny passages uncovered by the metering pin. Usually water here is terminal for the metering head. Sometimes, using a really good fuel additive like Wynns will break the water down into smaller molecules and let it get sucked through the metering head. You need a bit of luck!

Rust usually gets captured by the fuel filter. Get into the habit of writing the date and mileage in felt marker on the filter when it is replaced, so you can keep an eye on how old it really is.

If you replace any part of the system, air will need to be bled from the system, much like brakes. The fuel pump relay in the fuse box is set to allow about three seconds of running every time the ignition is turned on. This avoids flooding the engine if the ignition is left on. Repeatedly turning on the ignition for three seconds at a time will normally clear any air from the system.

NEVER remove the injectors and try bleeding, as a very fine high-pressure fuel mist will be sprayed over the engine. Any stray sparks will ignite it.

To test the individual injectors you need a Bosch or equivalent testing rig. The injectors fit into separate graduated glass tubes. As the air flap is opened, each individual injector's flow can be accurately measured. We gained 18bhp

on our Mk1 racer when we found that two injectors from a new boxed set only flowed the same at half-throttle as full-throttle. The mixture had been set correctly and looked fine before we tried this test. The injector rubber seals must be replaced every time they are removed, as they quickly go hard and may crack the housings when removing or refitting the injectors. Replacing the two poorly injectors got us a class record the following weekend. Take nothing for granted.

Modifying K-Jet systems

When the cylinder head and cam have been uprated, there is scope to modify the fuelling of a K-Jet car. On a Mk1, the first thing to replace is the throttle body. The secondary venturi is smaller on a Mk1 than on a Mk2, so simply retro-fitting the Mk2 is a simple and effective way to improve air flow. The Audi 5-cylinder engines are another cheap source of these throttle bodies. These need part of the Mk1 linkage fitting to work properly.

The inlet manifold must be relieved around the larger butterfly to allow the air to pass freely. Simply scribe around a new gasket to see what metal needs removing. Take care as it is fairly limited thickness. Luckily, the mounting bolt pattern is identical on all of the bodies. Weber used to make a single large butterfly but it was tricky to drive slowly, and it's rare now.

The next tweak is to fit an Audi or 16V rising rate warm-up regulator. These are easily recognised by the extra black pipe that leads to the inlet manifold. Under full throttle, extra fuel is allowed into the metering head by altering the fuel pressure, thus giving improved acceleration. The fittings are exactly the same as the original; all you need to do is fit a 'T' piece into the throttle body or inlet to get access to the vacuum that operates the regulator.

On most cars, that is all that needs attention, but there is a gain to be had by finding and fitting early Mk1 metering heads, as they flow more fuel because the fuel pin is different. Never attempt to strip the metering head – it's impossible to put back together again!

On race or competition engines that have to retain the 'original' K-Jet system, experimenting with alternative air flow sensors can be worthwhile. There are many different-shaped venturis from different K-Jet cars; Volvo 4-cylinder and others.

It's a time for experimenting on a rolling road to see the best set-up for your engine.

Surprisingly, the 16V parts do not work at all well on an 8V.

Catalytic converters had to be fitted for the American market, and some European markets, long before the UK, so there are odd in-between injection systems with the look of K-Jet but with some added electronics to protect the cat. These are best avoided, where possible, or converted to UK spec. A good example of this is the Golf 1-based Caddy Sport, introduced as a performance pick-up. It looked great but only had the same performance as the carburettor cars because it was so restricted by the injection. When we fitted a 1900 unit with all the right parts and ran it on the rollers, it was still 96bhp! Fitting the correct Mk1 GTI fuel system gave 140bhp. Say no more!

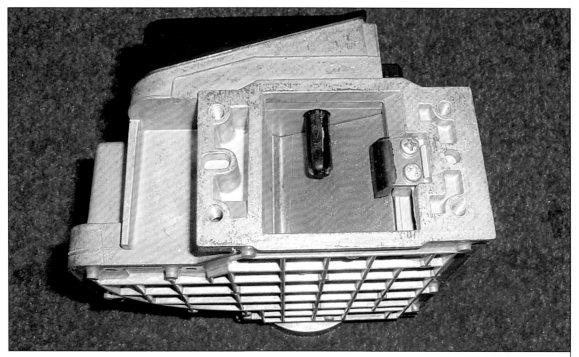

16V cars

The 16V Golfs ran with a straightforward K-Jet injection system, with different metering head and air flow sensors to suit the application. Many people think it is electronic simply because it runs an ECU. This ECU only controls the ignition, not the fuelling. Early pre-1989 cars had a smaller air filter than 1989 onwards cars. The warm-up regulator had the benefit of a vacuum operated enrichment system which is ideal for fitting to modified 8V cars.

Digifant injection

From 1986 VW introduced what has become known as Digifant (or Digi) injection. This was only fitted on Mk2 8V cars, the Mk1-based Cabrio and Scirocco and 16V retained the K-Jet system. This was an electronically controlled system with no parts interchangeable with the earlier K-Jet system.

The Digi system runs at lower pressure from the pump, the pressure being controlled by a small regulator fitted on the end of the fuel rail. The fuel rail also holds the electronic injectors. The quantity of fuel injected is controlled by the ECU, found under the edge of the windscreen in the engine bay.

The air filter is attached to the air mass sensor, basically a plate hinged at one end that gets moved by the air and keeps the ECU informed on the amount of air the engine is breathing, so that the ECU can give the corresponding fuelling via the injectors.

There are also throttle switches for full throttle and tick-over, and temperature switches for cold start, etc.

The often unreliable idle stabilising valve on 16V and Digifant cars.

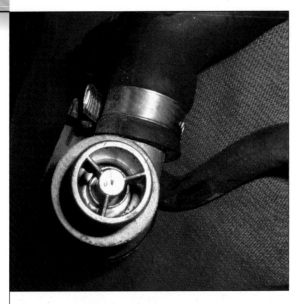

Idle stabilising valves can be cleaned with carburettor cleaner from this end.

A very common failure point was the idle stabilising air valve. It is a cylinder shape with an electrical connector on one end, and a pipe at the other. This moves constantly to keep the engine tick-over steady even with heavy loads from the alternator or power steering. It is common to suffer from high engine revs or surging if it fails. Initially, try cleaning the unit with carburettor cleaner, it gets very gummed up internally, especially on a high mileage smoky engine. Also, clean the throttle body and pipes the same way.

Abroad, this system was required to protect the catalytic converter from excess fuelling, but luckily not in the UK. The Digi system does not in itself make any more power than the original K-Jet system, so changing from one to the other is not an issue in modification terms.

The Digi system, with its control ECU does allow easy 'chip tuning' on the 8V cars.

The throttle butterfly is a large single unit, with micro switches fitted to feed information to the ECU. None of this needs modification on a tuned car. It copes well with major power increases with a simple chip replacement. As the ECU also controls the ignition advance and retard, the distributor is shorter (with no weights or springs) and is just a distributor of the sparks. The relevant Haynes Manual shows the correct procedure for setting the ignition advance.

Single-point injection systems

As a replacement for the original carburettors, a simple single-point injection system was used. All the VWs (except odd balls like the already mentioned Caddy Sports) that were made after the introduction of a catalytic converter, as has been said before, needed some form of injection to get the accurate fuelling needed to protect the cat and keep it in good condition.

This system was used on all the more mundane cars. It consists of electronic control via an ECU, controlling a single large injector inside what looks remarkably like a carburettor at a quick glance. The air filter even looks like the carburettor set-up.

This single-point injection system works well enough on a standard vehicle, but has very little extra fuelling available for a modified car. We spent ages trying to increase the fuelling potential on these cars when they first became available, with very little gain.

Basically, if you own one, DON'T persevere with serious engine mods, buy a multi-point injection model to start from.

On cars that were built and registered and were fitted with a catalytic converter from 1989 onwards, it is quite possible to remove the single-point system and cat, and retro-fit a carburettor from Weber, as the inlet manifold is very similar. It will also be necessary to fit the earlier ignition system too. This immediately gives lots of extra potential for serious power increases. Obviously, after 1992 'K' registration this is not legal as the cat is required by law.

Mk3 cars basically run a similar system, including the 16Vs. Apart from chipping, there is little that needs modifying on tuned engines. The lambda probe in the exhaust takes care of the monitoring of the mixture, and rechipping simply moves the 'goal posts' that the ECU can operate between.

In 1995, VW introduced a system of their own, called Simos. This was run in conjunction with the new immobiliser system. The key carried an internal chip that is recognised by the ECU via a sensor in the ignition switch. Initially, the engine will start but only remain running for about three seconds, unless the key is correctly recognised. The major components, including the dashboard wiring, of the injection system also recognise each other.

Replacing, say, an ECU with another will introduce a stranger and the car will not run. It's outside the scope of this book to go into details of the system, but basically be very wary of swapping these late components about from another car or you can end up with two cars not running!

If you buy a complete unit from a breaker to fit, 1.8T or VR6, make certain all the major components of the unit purchased come with it. The alternative (especially on a 1.8T) is to run a completely different aftermarket fuel system.

The VR6 also runs a Simos system on later cars.

To be able to read the stored information in the ECU via the diagnostic port, you will need a friend in the VW network or a well-equipped specialist garage.

It is advantageous on an early non-Simos VR6 Golf, to replace the original throttle body with a 2.9 Corrado item, as it is a larger diameter. No loss of torque will occur, and a few extra bhp will be available at the top end of the power range. The alternative item will bolt directly onto the inlet tract with no mods required.

Schrick also make an alternative complete inlet manifold intended to improve the low down torque of the VR6. It is a direct replacement for the existing inlet manifold, and cleverly uses a variable length inlet tract, or port, according to the engine's needs and revs. It is, however, quite expensive and may not be considered good value for money, as the power is not claimed to improve, just the torque. It largely depends on your driving style and attitude to initial throttle response.

Inlet manifolds

The cars need to retain the existing inlet manifolds, but all respond to careful gas-flowing, especially where the gaskets and ports meet. The internals are difficult to reach to polish beyond a certain point, and I doubt that there is much benefit to be gained anyway. Mk2 manifolds flow more air than a Mk1, as the inlet ports are larger.

A VR6 throttle body has one large butterfly. The 2.9 Corrado is larger and fits earlier cars.

The aftermarket carburettor manifolds need quite a bit of careful matching to fit snugly. Don't open the manifold up beyond the gasket line under any circumstances.

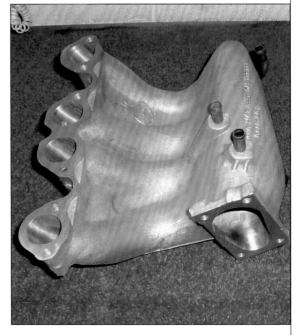

Another angle on an internally polished Mk1 inlet manifold, opened out to suit a bigger Audi throttle body.

ignition systems

The ignition system is a critical area for any engine, especially so in a modified unit. It is vital that the sparks are produced accurately and powerfully enough for full combustion to take place, especially at higher revs. Reliability is the key to a good ignition system.

Early 1100/1300 Golfs were blessed with a points system, with the distributor mounted on the end of the cam. The points tended to close up in use, and were difficult to set initially, as the distributor was awkwardly mounted and difficult to see into. Thankfully, the later hydraulic-cam models had a sealed electronic distributor fitted, which gives no problems in daily use. The two types have different distributor drives, so they will not easily interchange. As the early engine is not suitable for tuning anyway, it's not really a problem.

The 1500 and 1600 early cars were also equipped with points. The system is old-fashioned but reliable, and with points set correctly, and replaced at regular intervals, there was little to go wrong. There were several kits to replace the points and condenser with electronic ignition parts, but with the coming of factory-fitted electronic systems in the early 1980s it was better to simply replace the old points system with a complete electronic distributor and associated parts. It is a direct replacement.

1600 GTI models used a twin vacuum system, with two pipes to pull and push the ignition advance and retard, so simply use the suck side if you replace the distributor from a later car.

The distributors have a different static ignition timing and advance curve on the 1600/1800 Mk2 carburettor cars, so always use a GTI distributor, even on a carburettor car that has been modified. The advance curve suits the characteristics far better.

Use a second-hand GTI distributor and ignition amplifier, but also buy the wiring that connects the distributor to the ignition amplifier.

It is difficult to change the advance curve on electronic ignition cars, as it is controlled by the centrifugal weights in the base of the distributor. Altering these without a special rig, it is very much a case of trial and error, until you achieve the results you require. Generally the standard GTI distributor is fine, even on highly modified units.

There are two different types of distributor connection plugs on the cables from the ignition amplifier to the body of the distributor. They are easy to change, and can be bought cheaply from Bosch dealers.

A common tweak with high power output engines is to remove the vacuum pipe completely, and block the ends off. This stops the stronger vacuum from a modified engine sucking the advance in too quickly, and causing 'pinking'. The advance from the centrifugal weights still operates with the increase in revs, as normal.

It is common for VWs to suffer from 'pinking', even in mild states of tune. It can cause serious internal engine damage, so it is vital that if it occurs in your engine, you cure it quickly.

The Mk2 cars were all fitted with electronic distributors, but in 1985/86 the Digifant models gained an ECU to control both fuelling and ignition curve. These cars had a distributor that did not have any centrifugal weights inside. If you attempt to fit these distributors to an earlier car, you will have no advance at all. The later distributors are dumpier in height, and have square edges at their base.

This system was fitted to Mk3 cars also, but was replaced on Mk4s with coils fitted to each sparking plug. These are totally different in design, and will not interchange.

16V cars have a distributor mounted on the

Left to right: 2-litre Mk3 'tall block' distributor with larger gear, 1800 Digi, and earlier 1800 distributor with advance/retard in the casing.

exhaust cam, rather like a small-engine Golf. It, too, is simply a distributor, the advance is ECU controlled. The rotor arm is glued onto the centre shaft, and can be a grunt to remove. Take care to avoid bending the shaft.

If you fit a 16V engine to a Mk1, or 8V Mk2, make sure you either fit the correct ECU, or use a distributor with advance weights fitted. The easiest to fit is a Seat 1.2/1.5 Bosch distributor from a Systems Porsche early Ibiza. (Pre-1993). It has a reasonable advance curve and simply replaces the original 16V distributor. We have seen many conversions with no advance at all. This set-up is ideal if you want to run carburettors instead of an injection system, and don't wish to wire in the ECU.

The VR6 had two systems, both electronic and ECU-controlled. The early cars had a brown circular distributor cap, and a conventional set-up where the distributor did exactly that! It distributed the sparks in order.

The later cars had six coils, set in a pack, fitted in place of the distributor. The two

The later electronic distributors are shorter as there is no advance/retard mechanism.

systems will interchange, as long as the correct parts are fitted. The engine is the same, but the distributor drive is not needed and must be removed if you are using the later coil pack. The ECU is also different. The only reason to interchange these two systems would be to replace an early engine with a later one. They both work well.

An early VR6 distributor, later cars have a coil pack.

The 20V uses a separate coil on each plug.

20V engines

All 20Vs have individual complete coil packs on each plug. They are well known to cause trouble even when they are new, so check for problems here.

Distributor caps and spark plugs

When servicing an older non-ECU controlled car, remember to remove the rotor arm and lubricate the oil pad in the centre of the shaft. It is quite common to find strange advance curves, or none at all, because the centre shaft has seized, thus stopping the weights moving the advance/retard.

The two types of rotor arm, with and without a rev limiter.

If you need to remove the distributor, get the engine on TDC then check the rotor points towards the mark on the edge of the distributor body. If it does not, turn the engine another full turn until TDC is reached again. Undo the clamp bolt and carefully remove the distributor. You will notice the rotor turns as it is extracted, as the drive gears are cut at an angle.

DO NOT SPIN the distributor when it's out. The shaft tends to have slack in it when it's not in the fitted position. It's natural to fiddle, but it can cut the tiny wires under the timing rotor. Refit it allowing for the turning motion of the gears as they remesh.

The accuracy and reliability of the ignition system is affected by the state of the plugs and plug leads. Bosch and Beru make the majority of the standard plugs fitted in the VW network, and both are excellent quality. The later 3- and 4-electrode plugs of the correct grade are long lasting and vital to keep the cars ignition functioning correctly.

There are many aftermarket plugs available, but experience has shown that those purporting to give major power increases on their own, simply do not!

The plug leads must be up to standard spec, so check the resistance of each one against the original specifications. Again, there are many aftermarket sets available, and most are good in modified units. Most will not have the factory original steel shrouded caps, but use rubber instead. Many of the cars (VR6, etc.) have awkward ends to fit, and care needs to be taken when removing or fitting leads to avoid damaging the ends of the leads.

Aftermarket non-genuine distributor caps and rotors can be very inferior quality. I have seen clear caps (looks great) with incorrectly spaced contacts. Many of these spurious components are made in strange places far away with no real quality control, so take care to inspect them first.

Rotor arms

It's important to fit the correct rotor arm to your engine, avoiding spurious non-original examples! On the early 1600 GTI cars the rev limit is set by the rotor arm. Replacing it with a later solid 1800 rotor arm is a good idea if you need more revs.

Knock sensors and 'pinking'

No Golfs in the UK, except some imports, were fitted with knock sensors until the Mk2 models. They were then required because of the likelihood of increased 'pinking' due to the removal of lead and lower octanes when catalytic converters became mandatory by law. These cars with cats run on unleaded fuel, often of a lower octane.

Knock sensors have good and bad points.

The cars with ECU-controlled ignition advance/retard will not 'pink' if the knock sensor is working correctly. It hears the 'pinking' before the human ear (especially with the stereo turned up) and instantly removes some of the ignition advance, before the engine can be damaged. A VR6 on the rolling road will give a high bhp figure before dropping back a little as the knock sensor recognises the onset of 'pinking'. When fitting a knock sensor, take care to make sure the faces are clean, and torque to the correct figure. With the car on a diagnostic tuner, the ignition timing will generally retard if you tap the sensor with a spanner, gently!

Running a high quality, high octane fuel, Shell Optimax for example, is a good way to avoid premature 'pinking' and loss of power, especially on rolling road shoot outs and track days!

The lower the quality or octane of the petrol used, the more the knock sensor will retard the ignition, and the lower the power will get.

Unleaded fuels do not affect VWs at all, as the valve seats and valves are high quality, but the lowering of octane below the original requirements does merit our attention. All non-ECU controlled cars will 'pink' readily if lower octane fuels are used, and with no knock sensors fitted, damage is inevitable eventually. A simple electronic 'add on' will cure the problem, either 'K Star' or an alternative from C&R allows a different advance curve to be added to a centrifugal distributor. It intercepts the signal and alters it to the new curve.

Often the engine will run better than before,

A knock sensor in all its glory.

especially on 16V cars. It has the advantage that the curve can be modified later if the fuel changes quality again, or the engine is further modified.

'Pinking' can also be caused by engine oil getting into the breathers from a worn engine. The oil is drawn back into the induction side of the inlet tract, where it gets burnt with the fuel mixture. It has the effect of lowering the octane level of the petrol.

Fuse boxes

Not strictly ignition, but a common electrical problem area especially on Mk1 models, from the earliest right up to the last Cabrios in 1992. Most of these cars will have had strange electrical problems at some time in their lives. The fusebox suffers water ingress; the mass of cables leading from the bulkhead into the back of the fusebox effectively leads any water straight into the fusebox. The water becomes trapped between the three layers of the fusebox, causing shorts and strange internal connections never intended by VW's design engineers. The only repair is to fit a new unit, but take care to reroute the cables so that they have a small loop before leading up into the fusebox to ensure any errant water can drip off below the fusebox instead of being led straight into it.

There are many different types of clutch and flywheel fitted to the different models of the VW Golf. The 1300 had a conventional clutch, easily uprated by fitting a G40 Polo assembly. The much more common 1500, 1600 and 1800 cars, including all the GTI models, have a 'back to front' clutch. The diaphragm is bolted to the crankshaft; the flywheel then bolts to the diaphragm with six bolts, instead of the other way round as on a 1300 or Mk3 and later cars.

Clutch

The clutch is operated by a pushrod running in the centre of the mainshaft (described later in the gearbox section). Always replace the bush and seals if the box is out. The design allows gearbox oil to get directly fed into the clutch if the bush is worn or the seals are in poor condition.

The pushrod bears on a very hard button in the centre of the circular plate. If the shaft is bent or the bush worn, the pushrod can push off-centre and actually miss the button completely. It will eventually drill through the circular plate if this occurs.

All the Mk1 and Mk2 clutches are cable

operated. RHD Mk1 Golfs and Sciroccos suffer from a built-in weakness in the cable operation, as the outer cable is only supported by the thickness of the bulkhead metal. LHD cars have a far better design; the outer cable is fitted securely into a sleeve in the steering column.

Always suspect the bulkhead is cracking if the clutch starts to creak or the pedal seems to be getting further and further away. Strong metal repair plates are available, with sticky backing to hold them in place. It's difficult to weld this area to repair the cracks because of the proximity of the soundproofing and wiring. When the engine is out, always have a good look as it's easy to get to then.

The Mk2s have no problems in this area. VW had learnt by then. The Mk3 cars had a simple hydraulic system with the introduction of the 02A gearbox.

All of the earlier clutches need a centralising tool to refit the clutch accurately. It is a plastic disc with a knob to centralise the centre plate. It costs very little to obtain.

The 1600 cars initially had a 190mm clutch but it was changed for a 200mm before the 1800 engine was introduced. The 200mm centre plate and diaphragm fits the 190mm flywheel.

The most common clutch is 210mm, but this has a nine-bolt flywheel. The whole assembly will bolt straight onto any of these model Golfs to uprate them. The flywheel bolts are different, so get them at the same time.

This standard 210mm clutch will easily cope with up to 140bhp, but a torquey engine will make it slip as the clamping pressure of the diaphragm is not high enough. A 16V diaphragm will clamp an otherwise standard clutch tighter.

The 16V cars share the same fittings, but the centre plate has a larger shaft and different number of splines, to suit the different 16V mainshaft. Some Seats and Mk3s run this clutch centre plate even as 8V cars.

Uprating clutches

There are several well-known clutch manufacturers making uprated clutches. We favour Black Diamond. They have largely taken the market with the inability of Sachs to supply

their excellent uprated road car clutches. The Black Diamond clutches run uprated crush springs and more clamping pressure to avoid clutch slip. They come with the big circlip and centre plate. The 210mm Black Diamond Golf clutch will stand up to about 180bhp and increased torque, but beyond that, a race set up is required.

The race spec 'paddle' clutch is metallic surfaced. On a road car it's very difficult to cope with, as it's virtually impossible to slip the clutch in traffic, as it's in or out! This is a serious competition unit only.

Opposite: A Black Diamond heavy duty 210mm clutch assembly and centre cover.

Mk1 bulkheads can rust or crack if the drainage holes are neglected or the clutch cable is very stiff. For cracks a repair plate is available.

A Black Diamond uprated clutch diaphragm for a VR6. (*Black Diamond*)

A Black Diamond centre plate for a VR6.
(Black Diamond)

At this state of tune, especially on very high torque supercharged or turbo units, it is time to fit the conventional type of G60 flywheel and clutch. This will only fit in an 02A/02J gearbox, but this too is stronger. The flywheel fits directly onto the crank. It is larger diameter and stronger and suits hard usage well.

Uprated clutches are available for all the VR6 models and 1.8T, though they are not required until the engines produce lots more power.

Flywheels

The weight of a revolving flywheel helps an engine to tick over evenly and smoothly. Unfortunately, it takes power to accelerate the flywheel. It has the same effect on the car as greater car weight.

All VW flywheels are suitable for lightening, as all carry excess weight. Obviously the nearer the weight is to the outside of the flywheel, the more it appears to weigh.

Removal of metal can be carried out anywhere except surfaces that support the clutch or crank. It is especially easy on all the Mk1/2 16V flywheels.

Several pounds can be removed in a lathe from a 210mm flywheel, right up to the ring gear. Rebalancing is essential if you lighten any flywheel.

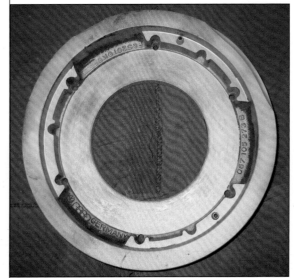

It's easy to lighten a Mk1 or Mk2 flywheel to good effect.
(Justin Napper/ TSR Performance)

gearboxes

Golfs have a range of three different gearbox types according to engine size. They have a type code that can be found on the casing. The type code is not the same as the individual gearbox code that is generally found on the lowest part of the clutch housing.

The smallest engines, 1100 and 1300cc, are fitted with a 084/5 type gearbox, and some early cars will still retain a 4-speed gearset. Fitting a later 5-speed gearbox is a simple substitution exercise. This gearbox is totally different from that on a larger-engined Golf, and the two will not interchange because the small-engined cars have a leaning back engine, while the larger cars have a leaning forward engine, so, apart from anything else, all the fittings are different.

The best version of this gearbox, and certainly the strongest fitted to an original car by the factory, is the rare G40 gearbox. There are no problems with retro-fitting this box to an earlier vehicle, as long as the gear linkage is also substituted at the same time. Generally, 4-speed gear linkage is different from 5-speed. You can modify it to get the extra movement required, but this is tricky and it's easier to fit the correct parts first time. The gearbox mount will also need to be correct. The gearbox to engine fitting is the same, though, so no drama there.

Always use the correct flywheel and clutch to suit the gearbox, i.e. the G40 gearbox requires a G40 clutch and flywheel. If you are buying it second-hand, then simply buy both parts from the same car. Some flywheels are the same anyway, but always make a physical inspection if you can. Better safe than stuck on a Saturday afternoon with incorrect parts.

The most common Golf gearbox is fitted to all the 1600 and 1800 cars, and some earlier 2-litre models. This is the 020 type, with rod linkages operating the gear change. The 020 type was available in a large number of different ratios. Essentially there are either close ratio or wide ratio gearsets in these boxes. I will ignore any of the few remaining 4-speed boxes, built before about 1979 in Mk1 Golfs, so we can concentrate on the more common boxes. The 5-speed is a straight substitution for the 4-speed, anyway, as long as the mounts and linkage are changed at the same time.

In use, this gearbox is strong and durable, with probably the best 'feel' of any VW gearbox. It will generally stand power up to about 180bhp, but dislikes high torque inputs from supercharged or turbo diesel engines. Its weaknesses are centred around the location of the diff pins. When they are loose, the danger sign is a 'tick' from the gearbox when rolling slowly forwards, as the pin catches in the casting. This is a terminal condition and the diff MUST be replaced immediately, or the casing will be ruined. Often the first thing you know about the failure of the diff pin is the clutch slipping and a small pool of oil under the car. It's too late! The pin has rubbed through the casing, and at some point it will smash a hole through the casing and release the gearbox oil onto the clutch, or ground. This is not practically repairable without fitting an alternative gearbox. The moral here is to test for the 'tick' at low speed (with your stereo off), if you run a modified engine. It's an unpredictable failure; some never break, some fail at low mileages. But fitting a limited slip diff removes this problem, as there is no diff pin.

Noisy fifth gears are a danger sign of either low oil levels, or failure of the bearing supporting the fifth gear. Either way, its expensive and repair requires the box to be removed.

Wear on second gear synchromesh shows as an unpleasant crunch when second is selected. This is particularly noticeable when the gearbox oil is cold, and it is generally improved on a long journey or in hot weather. It's not going to break anything but it's a sign of a tired gearbox. It's usually a good excuse to strip the box to rebuild it and fit a limited slip diff! If the problem is not too bad, simply drain the gearbox to remove the thick EP80/90 and refill with proper synthetic gear oil, and often it will improve the second gear dramatically, as it is thinner and does not baulk the synchro cone in the same way as the thick oil does.

There is a weakness, too, in the finger that operates the pushrod running through the inside of the mainshaft. These fingers are prone to cracking across the shaft. It's easy to replace as the finger is under the end-cover of the gearbox. The symptom of this failure is an inability to disengage the clutch even though there is plenty of movement in the cable and clutch arm.

Ratios

The 020 gearbox is available for many different applications. There is a big difference in the final drives according to the rev considerations of the original engine. Obviously, a diesel will need a very long or high ratio gearbox to make up for the low engine revs attained with a diesel engine, say 100mph at 4,000rpm. Conversely, a revvy unit like a 16V will require a short final drive gearbox with a diff to suit, say 100mph at 6,000rpm. If you interchange these gearboxes, for example, you get a diesel that will only do 75mph, and a 16V that will only get as far as third gear. Thus final drive ratios affect top speeds. Generally they will interchange within the limits of 020 gearbox casings, thus giving you a choice of gearing to suit your application.

It's vital to be clear about what you are trying to achieve, as gearing incorrectly will ruin or make the driveability of a car.

If you have modified the engine for more power, then your car will have the potential for a higher top speed, or you may simply require more acceleration. The rule generally is, the more acceleration the lower the ratios, or the higher the top speed the higher the ratios. If you are using the car for weekend motorsport, you will need to retain at least the original ratios to keep the top speed realistic, but if motorway cruising is to be restful, and economy is important, then by all means raise the final drive ratio.

Standard cars are very well sorted by VW themselves. It's all compromise.

The gaps between the gears are also very important. Ideally, we all want a close ratio gear cluster for any sporting or fast road applications. The standard ratios are really quite acceptable for most people, but you can change them to suit your needs. Again, be sure what you really need.

Lowering the final drive ratio will close up any gear cluster ratios, but it will also make top speed noisier and at higher engine revs, thus less fuel efficient. This is probably all right for weekend motorsport cars. Raising the final drive ratio will have the opposite effect.

The easiest and closest ratio standard gearbox is the early 1600 GTI gearset; we use it for most of the club level cars, and sprint/hillclimb cars. As a standard package it's easy to source and is reliable and cheap, although one of the bearings is hard to source now. This gearbox will not fit a Mk2 car, as the driveshaft joint is larger, and Mk2 boxes have a cut-out to accommodate this. It's actually a useful way of recognising the difference between a Mk1 and Mk2 box.

The next best is the 1800 GTI gearbox, followed by the 1800 Mk2 and 16V. Remember, many of these boxes are old and tired now, so simply fitting an unrebuilt unit from a breaker's yard can be a gamble. They are not difficult to strip and rebuild, and the bearings, etc. are cheap, so it's down to you. It's a day's hard work to strip, inspect and rebuild a box.

The 16V gearbox has a few differences from an 8V box; a larger mainshaft, and different internal bearings to suit the larger shaft, but while they interchange directly, you must fit the correct clutch centre plate to suit the different mainshaft sizes. The clutch covers are the same, except the clamping pressure is higher on the more powerful 16V.

If your 16V gearbox expires, simply fit the Mk2 8V box and clutch centre plate, they are cheaper and virtually the same ratios, and far more plentiful second-hand. Some 8V and 16V Seat Ibiza/Cordoba fitments are the same as 16V Mk2s too.

Surprisingly, maybe, the 8V box seems less troublesome than the supposedly stronger 16V box.

While you have your gearbox on the floor, always replace the two oil seals on the output flanges of the diff, as they are very prone to leaking. Also check the pushrod that operates the clutch mechanism for straightness and burrs, and then replace the small pushrod bronze bush inside the hollow mainshaft. It's easily removed with a suitable tap. Now replace

the seal on the shaft too. An oil leak here carries gearbox oil straight onto the clutch centre plate.

It is possible to simply replace fifth gear for a longer or shorter ratio set (even with the box still in place) by dropping the end of the box down, and replacing the two parts of fifth gear.

Wide ratio boxes

VW carburettor and diesel cars usually have the widest ratio gearboxes on standard models, to give effortless cruising at low engine revs. With a higher top gear the gaps between the ratios in the intermediate gears will widen. This is ideal for those who are modifying their cars for more power and torque, and want to use them for high mileages and are seeking fuel efficiency.

Fitting one to a standard car generally ruins it, and cars with high power outputs (at high revs) will also be short of the bottom-end grunt necessary to pull a wide ratio box, especially 16Vs.

It's a straightforward job fitting a pair of fifth gears from a long box, even without removing the gearbox, and this can be ideal for those who are willing to put up with first to fourth gears being close ratio, with fifth as a cruising only gear. I had this on my own hillclimb/sprint

Fitting the replacement fifth gear set with the gearbox in place.

car, using only the close ratio gear cluster for competition and keeping fifth gear for the drive home after events.

Alternative gear clusters

There are many alternative gearsets available, but virtually all are only suitable for the 02A/02J type of cable change boxes.

I ran an 020 early gearbox with an ultra close ratio set-up, where first gear was extremely high, making it difficult to get off the line on any slight slope. I believe these gearsets are now only available second-hand. The 02A/02J boxes are well catered for, though.

The most common conversion has to be the excellent Quaife 6-speed. It is supplied with a special casing to extend the fifth/sixth gear end of the box. It is suitable for either overdrive sixth or close ratio sports use, as several final drive ratios are available to suit the usage.

The sequential gearchange from Sequishift will also work well with this set-up, although you must order the Sequishift to suit the 6-speed box, as there is one more movement position.

The newest 6-speed gearsets actually come from Sequishift themselves. They make two different sets of gears. First, the Comfort variant which consists of a shorter ratio fifth and an overdrive sixth gear, and parts to fit the 02A/02J box. This is cheaper and suits road cars best, but obviously after they have been modified to produce more power or torque. The second, and far more comprehensive, kit has new third, fourth and fifth gears with shorter ratios, then a special sixth. So, really the sixth is where fifth was before, thus making a very close ratio gearset, but reusing your original first and second gears. This is superb in a revvy engine – 1.8T or VR6. It's

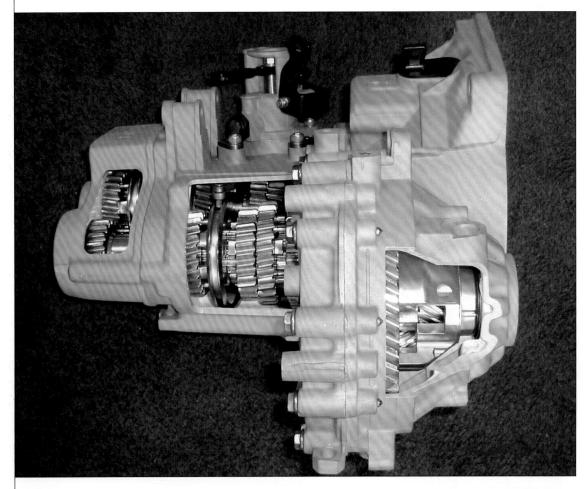

The superb 6-speed gearset and limited slip differential from Quaife.

also the set-up to retro-fit to a very well modified Mk2.

A word of warning here about fitting any 6-speed gearbox into a Mk1. As the 6-speed gearbox is obviously now longer than the original 5-speed box, it will foul the inner arch and restrict the right-hand steering lock. You have been warned!

Quickshifts for 020 boxes

Quickshifts are available for all gearboxes but they will not make tired linkages tighter! VW made a bit of a meal of the linkages on the 020 gearbox. They are complex and get badly worn in use. First, rebush the linkages with a rebushing set from VW – they are cheap and will keep you occupied for hours. Then, and only then, fit a quickshift if you wish. Mk1s and Mk2s are totally different and won't interchange. Although the gearboxes are similar, the linkages are different.

Mk1s

The idea is to shorten the fore and aft movement of the gearlever, to make your gearchange more rapid and precise. There are two ways to do this: one is to simply shorten the vertical gearbox lever with a suitable kink if required to allow the linkage to clear it, and the other is to replace several links with different length sections. This allows not only shorter fore and aft movement, but also affects the sideways movement too. In practice, you need really good heavy duty engine and steering rack mounts to control the engine and rack movement, especially sideways, because the Mk1 has the gear linkage attached to the steering rack before connecting to the gearbox. So, in hard cornering the rack gets pushed in the opposite direction to that which you are turning. The engine's weight also pushes hard on the mounts, and the net effect is that in

The 6-speed conversion from Sequishift with the extended alloy cover for the extra gear. *(Sequishift)*

extreme conditions the linkage no longer lines up with the gear you are expecting. This is exaggerated with a Mk1 if you insist on the whole quickshift kit, as you have a smaller margin for error between the sideways movement available.

The other common but generally missed reason for a poor linkage, is the nut supposedly tightly holding the vertical link to the shaft. There is a D-shape that wears badly if the nut is loose. Simply tighten it and maybe spot a dab of weld to locate it if all else fails, but don't melt the nylon bush above it.

If you decide to remove a Mk1 linkage to rebush it, take care to mark the splined shaft so it can be replaced accurately afterwards, as it can be difficult to get right and seems to operate in the opposite direction to what you might think.

Mk2s

While there is a similarity with Mk1s, the actual system is far more reliable – with a couple of exceptions. If you can select reverse without pressing the gearlever down, then replace the ball and socket under the lever with a VW kit of parts. As the Mk2 has no connection between the rack and linkage, there are no real problems here, but all the bushes will need replacing regularly as they are quick to wear. Again, a kit of bushes from VW is not expensive and it's a good way to spend a day.

Fitting a quickshift is dead easy and consists of a shorter vertical gearbox link, often with two positions for the cross rod to fit into. The lower is the shortest movement, but we prefer to use the top hole. Obviously, heavy duty engine mounts will improve the feel considerably.

Linkages

Both Mk1 and Mk2, and some early Mk3/Seats, will be improved by replacing the plastic standard linkage with proper spherical jointed rods. These are available from TSR Performance at a price cheaper than VW standard replacements, and they simply clip on in place of the originals. Also they can, with care, be adjusted to suit individual applications to get really superb accuracy, and the best feel.

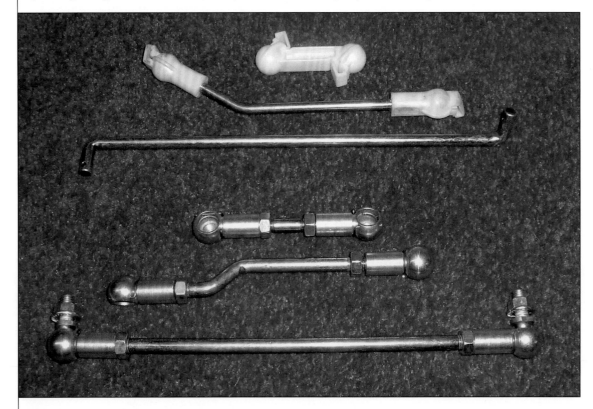

MK2 standard and TSR gear linkage kits.

Weighted cross rods are also available to give the linkage more feel. These are standard on Seats, or available aftermarket.

02A and 02J cable change gearboxes

The Passats were the first cars to use this completely new box, several years before they became Golf gearboxes, so they were well tested. Early ones are 02A, and later they had a slightly different diff and changed to 02J, but they are very similar. They are, though, totally different in all respects from the earlier boxes, both externally and internally. The linkage is also totally different, being cable operated, and this is really the weakest part of the system in everyday use. The earliest cars were often notchy and could be vague, but the system is far better now as it has been refined considerably from the early set-up. This also means that, if you replace the gearbox you need the correct linkage/cables/remote lever from the same car as the gearbox to get a happy set-up.

They are immensely tough and have none of the earlier 020 faults. The gears and bearings

A 02A gearbox fitted to a 20V engine. The end cover is a useful identifying feature.

The parts needed to recondition a tired 020 gearbox.

This alloy gear selector support can be easily uprated with a stronger steel bush on a competition car running an 02A/02J type of gearbox.

are well able to take any diesel or supercharged torque, even in standard form.

The ratios are much as the 020 boxes, the lower revving cars (supercharged G60s and diesels) had longer wider ratio boxes, while the sporty cars (16Vs, etc.) had close ratio lower geared boxes.

VR6s use the same basic 02A/02J boxes, but they have different block fitting at the clutch end, so will not fit anything except VR6s.

These boxes are certainly far more difficult to strip, as fourth gear is very tight on its shaft and can be easily damaged in removal. The correct removal tools are really useful here.

There is a potential slight problem with very hard used 02A boxes in the alloy support for the base of the selectors. This can be uprated with a steel replacement if required.

Retro-fitting 02A/02J to earlier cars

With the reminder that you need the correct cable mechanism to go with your gearbox if you buy a second-hand unit, it is feasible and generally desirable to retro-fit this strong

gearbox into earlier cars, if your car has a good deal of torque.

If a G60 supercharged unit or diesel is fitted to an older car, Mk2 or Mk1, then fit an 02A box too, and finish the job with a degree of strength built in.

The linkage is basically simple to bolt up in place of the old system, and the gearbox casing also bolts straight on to the engines with no hassle.

It is ESSENTIAL to fit the later flywheel and clutch to suit the gearbox you are using, as the clutch mechanism is completely different. It's quite simple to manufacture a linkage kit for Mk2 conversions, but Mk1 is harder.

The cable linkage can be converted on Mk2 or Mk1 to operate the previously hydraulic system with Seat parts and a Golf 1300 cable. A kit is available from TSR Performance.

The clutch is very conventional compared with the earlier 'back to front' 020 system, and it's also stronger and bigger in diameter. There is no pushrod running through the centre of the main shaft, so no more oil leaks. Diffs are immensely tough too.

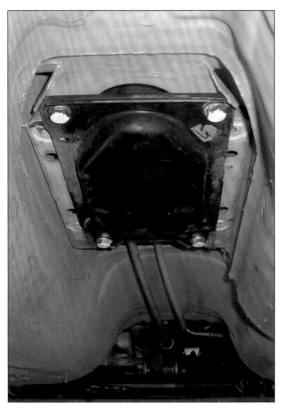

Far left: A Mk2 fitted with the cable change mechanism and 02A gearbox.

Left: The 02A/02J gearbox showing the hydraulic slave cylinder that normally operates the hydraulic clutch on the standard cars. It is possible to replace this system with a simple cable operation if the box is retro-fitted to an earlier car.

The 02A/02J box cable linkage from above showing the top of the selector shaft. The clamp bolt can come loose.
(Sequishift)

A B&M 02A/02J quickshift kit.

Quickshifts for 02A/02J

The quickshift set-up on 02A/02J is totally different from the older box too. As it is cable operated, it's difficult to convert, but B&M shifters are available from tuners and Eibach, who import them direct from the States in several types to suit the different ages and types of cable set-ups. These units are beautifully engineered to make the throw of the gearlever shorter, and thus quicker.

The fitting will require lifting the car, and sometimes the removal of the exhaust system is necessary to allow downward removal of the lever assembly.

A steel bush at the base of the box to replace the existing alloy piece is a good strengthening idea. It helps to support the base of the gearchange mechanism.

Sequential shifts 02A/02J

Recently, sequential gearshifts have become available, where the lever moves either forward for down the box or backwards for upward

Generally, use a G60 or Mk3 Golf 2-litre flywheel/clutch, as it's fine up to 200bhp. Heavy duty units are available. Again, you can't use any VR6 parts as they will not fit anything except VR6 blocks. Also, avoid T4 Transporter 02A second-hand, as the linkage is different and the boxes are usually harder worked in a big van.

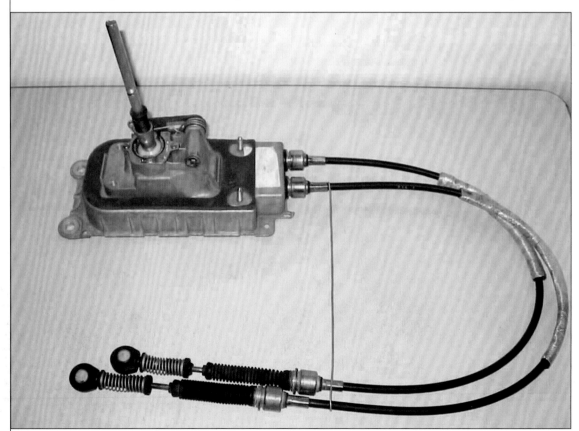

The cable change system from an 02A/J box. (Sequishift)

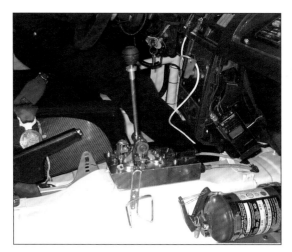

Top left: A Sequishift in place in a competition car mounted internally instead of underneath the tunnel. The cables are flexible enough to allow either fitment. On a rally car the mechanism is more protected inside the car and the lever is nearer to your hand on the steering wheel. *(Sequishift)*

Top right: Here is a Sequishift fitted in a road car. It fits under the floor in the original position. *(Sequishift)*

Turning the Sequishift unit over reveals the two operating rings that control the cables. *(Sequishift)*

changes. Reverse is avoided by means of a spring-loaded catch on the lever. This is expensive and copies the 'rally car' set-up used on all serious competition vehicles.

The fitting is not technically difficult but requires a bit of care setting up the cables afterwards. Early cable change boxes require the later cables and fittings, as these adjust individually. It's the ultimate for those who want the look and feel of a factory car. The linkage can be fitted underneath the car as originally, or inside to protect the working as on a competition car, since the cables are flexible enough to cope.

limited slip differentials and driveshafts

Limited slip differentials

Limited slip differentials (LSDs) totally transform a Golf with whatever gearbox you are running. There are two basic types available. Luckily, viscous coupling diffs (*à la* RS Turbo Escorts) are not available for VWs, so life is a bit safer!

First, there are competition plate LSDs from Gemini (now trading as Ricardo) consisting of many plates preset to a fixed torque, so they can slip under pressure.

These are expensive to produce, require muscles of iron to turn the steering wheel, and wear quickly in daily use. They need rebuilding at least yearly to retain the pressures. The plates rub and thus get thinner, so the pressure gradually drops. They are ideal for rough surface rally cars, as they are less prone to snatching the driveshafts, where the wheels are losing traction. They require different output shafts to fit the gearboxes, and are virtually twice the price of the alternative LSDs.

The second type is a great favourite of mine. The Quaife torque bias diff is a simple,

either in or out, gear-driven diff, dead easy in operation and suitable for road and competition vehicles.

The advantages of an LSD, especially the Quaife type, is that you get serious traction out of corners. As power is added, it tries to drive both wheels at the same speed, instead of spinning the unloaded one as the standard diff does. It allows you to pull the car out of the corner by adding power earlier. The LSD also stops the waste of wheel spin at the start of, say, a quarter-mile sprint, or a wet roundabout. On the 020 boxes it also removes the weak and problematical diff pin. It's really essential if you want good initial acceleration and the ability to pull the car out of tight corners.

A good LSD is by far the best value for money of virtually any tuning modification. Even standard cars benefit, as they can put all of their limited power down on the track. There's no point in having 200bhp and only being able to put half of it down with certainty.

Right and opposite (top left): Views of the plate limited slip differential from Sequishift. (Sequishift)

Driveshafts

All VW driveshafts are very strong and durable even under very hard use. The Mk1 had basically the same driveshaft and CVs right through the whole range from 1100 to GTI models. We used ancient 1100 driveshafts on our race/rally car with no problems with over 140bhp. All run 90mm inner driveshaft joints except later Mk1-based models from about 1986 onwards, Cabrios, Caddy and Sciroccos when VW used a 100mm inner joint to suit the Mk2 gearboxes that were then introduced. This joint is not the same as a Mk2 inner joint, so beware. The inner and outer CV joints will interchange easily as the shafts have the same splines.

Mk2 cars and later models have different length driveshafts, so will not interchange with the shorter Mk1 cars. Most of the Corrado and Mk2/3 models are the same lengths and so interchange between models.

For really serious racing applications there are Ricardo shafts available at considerable cost. Even stage rally cars will run standard driveshafts quite reliably unless the joints are subjected to extreme angles from the car's suspension being set too high, or the surfaces are causing full lock under full power to be frequently used.

The CV is the weakness, not normally the driveshaft, and it will eventually break the cage

that locates the balls, allowing them to slide out or jam, usually under full lock conditions.

I have seen the actual driveshaft snap off at the splines under extreme conditions. Make sure when assembling the CV to the shaft that the circlip and spacer are correctly seated and the CV really locates correctly on the shaft. I have seen the CV drop off on full suspension droop on a big 'yump' in a stage.

Those of you doing weekend motorsport or track days should be able to use standard driveshafts in most conditions, even with 200bhp and a Quaife LSD.

05 running gear

The Golf was a radical rethink for VW after the old Beetle, and the resulting improvement in handling was quite a surprise even on a standard early Mk1 1100 Golf. Come the sporty GTI versions, a further huge step was made in refining the handling with the addition of an anti-roll bar, better damping and slightly wider wheels. At the time the motoring press were amazed at the grip available, and even now the car is in a class of its own, a very successful compromise between handling and comfort.

Suspension

Surprisingly, all Golf's share a very similar suspension set-up, whatever age they are. Mk1, Mk2, Mk3 and Mk4 all have MacPherson struts at the front, and a substantial rear beam at the rear, but with numerous detail changes.

Mk1 models

As the original it's hard to fault. The car is considerably lighter than later cars, so it naturally handles the best. It is still the club level competitor's first choice.

There is no front subframe on a Mk1; the lower wishbones are attached directly to the chassis. This can be a potential weak spot, but it is quite easily strengthened by the addition of a cross brace, linking the lower wishbone bolts together. This is a very good tweak, especially if the car has bigger wheels and tyres, as the additional grip can cause flexing of the inner mounts. Later Sciroccos and Cabrios had strengtheners fitted from the factory.

The basic shell is amazingly strong and does not require any serious strengthening unless it's being used off road. Obviously, a serious rally car will have been fitted with a full cage, and then it's sensible to add supports to the top of the front and rear turrets for extra strength, but

this is really beyond the scope of this book.

The rear beam is a huge and heavy single unit that acts as a torsion bar by bending under load. Looking at it, you could be forgiven for doubting its bendability, but bend it surely does. Look at a photo of a hard driven Mk1 – it shows, though you cannot feel it inside the car. The rear beam will often lift the inside wheel well off the ground under hard cornering. It's spectacular, but normal!

Both front and rear suspension share a 'coil-over' system, with coil springs fitted over the dampers. It's very effective in use, cheap to modify and simple to work on. The front dampers bolt onto the front hubs by two bolts. The top bolt is adjustable to allow camber changes to be made.

All Mk1 GTIs are fitted with anti-roll bars as standard. These simply add roll resistance to the front and rear suspension, transferring the loads from the side under the heaviest load to the unloaded side by means of a torsion bar, and greatly improving the 'feel' and stability of the car for the driver. They are a direct retro-fit to non-GTI models, as long as the brackets are bought with the anti-roll bars. Two holes will need drilling in the wishbones to fit the front brackets, and the rear beam clips are difficult to refit, so buy new ones to keep life simple. The anti-roll bars must be fitted as a matched pair, or the car will be unbalanced.

The top suspension mounts are bonded rubber. These can perish badly, so it's a good idea to always replace them (see section on modifications in this chapter). The simple test is to try to fit a ball-point pen or little finger under the top plate. If the gap is that large, then replace them because stiffer springs will force them further apart very rapidly, and they can also fail the MoT test if they are in poor condition.

At the rear, the beam is bolted to the body via two large rubber bushes that bolt onto brackets attached to the box section on the floor. Take care to check this area of the chassis very carefully if your car is at all rusty, as it's a serious and difficult area to repair, requiring the removal, or at least the dropping of, the rear beam, and petrol tank. It is not an easy place to weld a repair plate. Usually, it's better to use a better shell in the first place. The external 'give away' to this problem is rust along the lower section to the outer sills, so have a good look first.

Mk2/Mk3 models

As far as the suspension is concerned, these models are virtually the same as a Mk1 to work on, as they share similar basic components.

The main differences from a Mk1 are:
- There is a supporting cross member linking the lower wishbones on both models. This acts as a substantial strengthening for the front suspension, and also supports such vital elements as the steering rack and engine. It can become very tatty, and can suffer serious structural rust on the rare cars with oil-tight engines. A careful inspection is vital, especially when the front wishbones are removed.
- The front dampers bolt onto the front hubs as on a Mk1, but without the adjustable camber set-up, although camber adjustment is still possible.
- The cross member is attached to the car by rubber bushes, front and rear. These, too, suffer from old age and can be uprated.

The two large bolts that go through the rear rubber bushes and wishbones can rust into the captive nut in the chassis, causing major headaches if they are disturbed with too much force. It's quite easy to shear the captive nut off inside the front chassis leg, requiring a hole to be made to get to it from the inside of the car. It's difficult and time consuming. Always soak the area well with WD40 before you attempt to remove the bolt.
- The rear beam is similar in design to the Mk1, but different in shape, and the rear anti-roll bar is fitted inside the rear beam on the GTI models only. Thus, you can't retro-fit the basic non-GTI cars, diesels and carburettor models, with a rear anti-roll bar, unless it's an aftermarket kit. The front bars will easily fit, but the balance is terrible with only a front bar fitted.

The Mk3 cars share many of the same parts as a Mk2, but the sporty models, with 5-bolt wheels, have wider track and a different PLUS axle beam. This has different and firmer bushes. The front wishbones are wider to match the rear beam width, and the wishbone bushes are fitted in a different manner too.

Be careful if you try to fit some Mk3 suspension parts to Mk2s, they increase the track of the car, and then generally the wheels catch the arches on bumps.

Mk4 models

The Mk4 has many differences from the previous vehicles. The front struts do not simply bolt onto the front hubs, but locate by sliding into the hub and thus have non-adjustable camber. This is common to many of the other cars based on the same chassis as the Golf 4 – Skoda Octavia and Beetle, etc. It can be difficult to remove older struts, as they get rusty, so a liberal dose of WD40 before you tackle the job is advisable.

At the rear, it's also all change. The rear dampers and springs are separate units, not coil-overs, and the beam is different as well.

Basically, the suspension components will not interchange between the earlier models and the Mk4s.

Modifications
Fitting lowering kits

There are a vast number of possibilities here, with so many kits of dampers and springs available, from cheap to expensive (manufacturers' warranties can vary a great deal too). My experience is that the better kits allow more adjustment and usually have far better ride quality.

Fitting springs on their own can be a disaster, certainly on the older cars. Springs alone simply alter the ride height, so it looks better and moves the centre of gravity closer to the ground, but achieving good suspension is an exact science, and much more complicated than simply swapping springs.

It is far more cost-effective and will give a far better ride, if you replace the damper first, as this will improve the handling without compromising anything, especially the ride quality.

Use variably rated springs of high quality, Eibach for example, as these alter their spring rates according to the load carried, or cornering loads. The effective length of the spring decreases with increased load. As the coils close up against each other they make the spring stiffer in order to cope with the increasing loads. This also helps to stop bottoming out the dampers over bad road surfaces.

The dampers are there to damp the spring's natural movement, as the name suggests, so fitting springs with a shorter length will call for better, quicker acting dampers. Old and tired dampers will not damp the frequencies produced by a set of lowered springs, so please try to replace the dampers first, or together with the spring kit.

All the models will benefit from fitting a lowered suspension kit. The trick is recognising the correct height for your needs. If you have a show car, and it will not be an everyday driver, you can afford to go lower than an everyday road car can. The real secret is to fit a 'ride height adjustable' kit, as this allows complete freedom, and can be set at the height best for the occasion. It will require resetting (for camber and tracking) if the front height is altered.

Basic non-adjustable kits

Many kits come with the springs lowered by about 30/40mm, and with gas dampers like Boge, etc. These are superb value; they are easily fitted and transform the look and handling of all models. Generally, gas dampers are firmer and non-adjustable (for hardness), whereas the coil-over gas units, like Koni, allow hardness adjustment.

To fit these kits will need a spring compressor. They are not expensive, but require good workshop practice in use or serious injury can occur. Never try to remove a spring without understanding how to use the correct equipment. A compressed spring is a dangerous object. Never leave it unattended on a workshop floor, as it contains a vast store of energy trying to escape. Always refit it as soon as it is possible. Always fit new bumpstops and top mounts at the same time.

All Golfs built before 1989 have struts that allow replacement of the internals (called inserts) alone. The strut casing that carries the damper has a removable threaded cap that unscrews (in theory!) to allow the damper to be extracted. Replacement inserts are available from several companies, including Boge and Koni. The old damper caps will normally need considerable force (and application of WD40), a large pair of grips or Stilsons and the use of a decent vice to persuade them to release. Years of mud and water will have rusted the caps in place.

If you find the threads are damaged, be wary of buying second-hand struts, as early struts (pre-1980) have parallel springs and the spring platforms are also different.

All the parts will interchange from other Mk1-based cars – Sciroccos, etc.

From late Mk2 onwards the struts have to be replaced completely, as the cap is welded not threaded. This is quite OK on earlier cars if the fitting of inserts is too awkward, but a bit more expensive.

Ride height kits

The ultimate kits are ride height adjustable. They will give far more suspension travel than a lowered spring kit. To lower the car, the actual base of the spring is lowered (the spring stays the same length), and the rule is: the longer the spring, the better the ride.

These kits are generically known as 'coil-over' kits, but that's true of virtually all standard suspension. They allow raising (rally cars) or lowering as you choose. Most good kits also allow adjustment to be made to the damping rates to suit your tastes, often by means of a top adjuster (Koni) so you don't need to grovel under the car. The adjusting rods need a bit of movement from time to time to keep the adjustment free and unseized.

They are fitted exactly the same way as the more basic kits, but you will need to spend some time getting even heights on the four corners. On a race car, this would be done with weight gauges, measure the load on each corner with the driver/fuel, etc. in the car, but it's not often practical on road cars, as they are driven with different loads, but it's a nice piece of theory anyway.

Top mounts

The top mounts, as mentioned before, are very prone to failure in use, especially as they support all the weight and movement of the whole front end of the car. Uprating the front suspension will increase the wear, as it's firmer and the pressure from the harder front springs will be greater too. The top mounts are similar in design throughout the Golf range, but will not interchange.

The Mk1 has the poorest design. The bonding of the rubber is rather weak, so only use factory or decent replacements, and don't forget the separate spacer inside the mount. It does not come with a new one! Alloy and uprated poly mounts are available, but they are also harder and sometimes harsh on a road car.

Mk2s have a better design. The G60 supercharged cars have a harder and stronger top mount in standard form, so this is the one to fit to modified road cars. These are quiet and pleasant in daily use. Aftermarket units are available in both alloy and poly.

Mark 3s and 4s share the same slightly stronger fitment. This seems strong enough in standard form, even for sports requirements.

A Mk2 with Koni ride-height adjustable suspension fitted.

Anti-roll bars

The idea of anti-roll bars is to carry the load from the compressed side of the suspension to the unloaded side via a stiff bar. It's a torsion bar. All sporty Golfs have front and rear anti-roll bars fitted as standard, from the first Mk1s to the latest cars, but carburettor and diesel cars (except some GL models) were generally not fitted with them. Have a look first, they may already be there. If your car corners like a 2CV, they are probably not fitted. As previously mentioned, they will retro-fit to all models if the correct brackets are fitted too.

Eibach make the best known anti-roll bar aftermarket kits. They are a superb fit and massively improve the chassis on any Golf. They come with the required brackets, poly bushes

Details of an Eibach anti-roll bar on a Mk2 rear. It simply attaches to the exterior of the rear beam.

slip diffs have only rear anti-roll bars fitted to make them very tail happy, so it's easier to change direction.

An anti-roll bar will also give a slight improvement in traction, as it keeps both front wheels more controlled, and tends to avoid the unloaded wheel spinning quite so much.

Poly bushes

Poly bushes must be the buzz word of recent years. They simply replace the rubber bushes wherever they were found in the suspension. The poly bushes are harder and stronger, but sometimes noisier. To stop them squeaking in summer, in dry weather, use a squirt of WD40 or special grease (antislip).

On Mk1s poly bushes are available for wishbone bushes, steering rack, rear beam and some engine mounts. They will all work well, especially the steering rack bushes, as they also help check the rack's sideways movement under hard cornering, thereby improving the gearchange. Fitting the rear axle bushes is fairly hard work, but well worthwhile. Anti-roll bar bushes will help with standard diameter bars only, as Eibach bars already have them as standard.

and fittings. They are quite a struggle to fit on a Mk1, easier on Mk2s and 3s, and you will struggle with the front bar on a Mk4 as it is a very tortuous shape indeed. Take care, especially on early Mk 4s when replacing the roll bars or lowering the car, that the steering arm does not make occasional contact with the anti-roll bars. An alternative drop link is sometimes required.

Fitting a rear only anti-roll bar can aid turn-in on a circuit car (it's also ideal for track days) if you have not got a limited-slip diff. Simply disconnect the link ends and leave the bar in place to avoid complete removal at track days and sprints. Some racing cars without limited-

The bushes make a great difference to a Mk2, as it's got more rubber in its mounts in the first place, thus more potential for excess movement. The best and most important replacements are the rear bushes in the front wishbones. Fitting poly bushes here largely stops the excessive fore and aft movement of the standard bushes. A car on the rolling road shows this really clearly if you accelerate and lift off quickly. The movement backwards and forwards is surprising, and affects the camber and tracking greatly. The car will have vastly better handling after fitting just these two bushes.

There is a slight difference between the Mk2 and Mk3 bushes, so be sure to fit the correct part. The Mk2 uses a thin sleeve to locate the bolt, so the centre tube is different. Vibratec make an excellent heavy duty rubber replacement for the same job, as an alternative to fitting a poly bush.

Two poly bushes are available for non-power-steering racks, while power-steering cars have

A Mk1 with Koni suspension kit and Eibach anti-roll bars really handles.

FDE 964W

the rack bolted directly to the subframe and consequently don't need any. Poly bushes are also available for the subframe and the radiator cross member. Rear axle poly bushes are excellent, too, but there are two sizes – the later one is known as a plus axle and it's fitted to the 5-bolt wheel equipped cars only. Standard size anti-roll bar poly bushes are available as well.

Wishbones

The Mk1 front wishbones are quite weak in use (I have bent many while rallying and racing) but they are easy to strengthen. Box in the two slots with a flat piece of steel, welded continuously, on both sides of the wishbone. At least they are a weak point, often saving chassis damage in an accident, and very easily replaced.

Mk2 and 3 wishbones will bend, too, in competition use and are far harder to replace, as they also help to locate the subframe. Strap them, or continuously weld them. They can rust out! Check them while they are off and replace the bushes if necessary.

Bumpstops

The primary function of bumpstops is to protect your dampers from damage when you go over a big hole in the road and the suspension reaches the shortest part of its travel. Remember, the available travel is considerably less on a lowered car, so they may well come into action far more

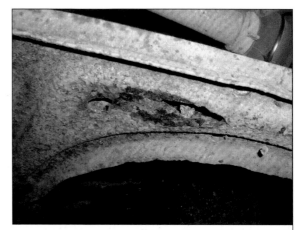

A very rusty and dangerous Mk1 lower wishbone. They are cheap and easy to replace.

Mk2 front wishbone bushes. Right to left, standard VW, Poly and Vibratec.

than intended originally. Make sure that the weight of the car does not rest on the bumpstops, or they will not last long.

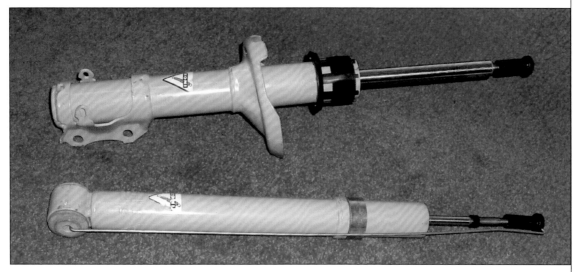

A Koni suspension kit can transform the handling of a Golf.

The factory front bumpstops are pretty good, but the rear foam types are useless when they get old. Replace them with later new factory units or harder aftermarket units in proper rubber compound.

A secondary function of a bumpstop is to act as a suspension travel limiter. It can stop excessive wheel travel where there is limited space, e.g. a lowered car, where the tyres foul the arches on bumps or with a heavily loaded car. Very careful measuring is needed to get maximum travel but still allow the bumpstop to arrest the suspension movement before the tyre hits the arch.

Special hard rubber bumpstops can be fitted to the rear damper on Mk1, 2 and 3 models, but not Mk4s as the suspension is different. The Mk4s have far more available space in the rear arches, so mods here are largely unnecessary.

To fit modified rear bumpstops, first remove the wheel, then the complete damper, and take the rear spring off. Refit the damper loosely in place with the wheel on. Measure the minimum distance on the piston shaft that will allow the wheel/tyre combination to avoid touching the arch. Cut the bumpstop slightly longer than that, so that it comes in contact just before the tyre hits the arch.

Replacing the suspension

Jack up the car safely, using axle stands to support the car, not just a jack.

Before taking off the front struts, mark the camber bolts (Mk1 only), then remove the bolts attaching the hub to the base of the struts. Undo the top mount, by two bolts (Mk1), or by removing the plate (Mk2, 3 and 4), and unclip the brake line.

Take the complete unit to the vice and compress the front spring, taking care at all times that the hooks have located around the coils and the two parts of the compressor are equidistantly apart. Compress the spring equally on both sides, and check the top plate is just free before removing the plate. It is located with a nut on a Mk1, but a special tube-shaped tool is required on the other later models. Many full suspension kits have one in the kit. If not, make or buy one, as it is vital. If you are fitting new springs, remove the compressors with great care.

Fit the new strut into the vice gently (do not crush it, as this will distort the piston or tube), then carefully compress the new spring until it is just short enough to fit the strut and allow the top plate and nut to be done up. The spring will be shorter, so it will not need so much compressing to refit it. Fit new bumpstops and top mounts at this stage. It is false economy not to do this. If the kit is lower than 40mm, slightly shorten the bumpstop, or the travel will be too short, and the bumpstop will act as a suspension spring until it splits and falls off!

Remove the compressor and relax. Refit the strut in a sequence opposite to that of removal, explained above.

When it is all refitted, reset the camber and tracking to suit (probably a professional job), and start on the rear. Remember the Mk4 is different, but similar in principle.

The rear is easier. Jack up the car, using axle stands under the body, not under the beam. If you support the car under the beam, it stops the rear beam from moving downwards, thus making removal of the rear dampers impossible.

Make sure you use the correct place to support the weight, as most of the bodywork and sills are not meant to support the car's weight. There are proper jacking sections built into all the cars, strong enough to take the weight of the car.

Remove one side at a time or the beam will fall down. Undo the lower bolt, and then the upper nut and plate on the top of the damper from inside the rear of the car. You will need to remove the plastic speaker shelf first.

Remove the whole damper unit complete, and undo the top nut on the damper. No spring compressors are needed as there is very little tension on this spring. Refit the new units, being careful with the collar with a groove in it. There is a small circlip that must locate inside the groove in the collar, if you fit it the right way up!

Check the rear spring locating plate for rust before refitting it.

Refit the complete unit to the car, and do the other side. There is no adjustment needed to the suspension angles.

If you have adjustable dampers, set the rears to a low setting, and the fronts to, say, $1/3$ of the max setting for a starting point. Too firm will give a strange ride. You can raise the damping rate for track days to increase the firmness.

Camber, castor and tracking

The accurate setting up of the car is vital, as it affects so much of the way the suspension works. Really wide low-profile tyres will not allow more than $\frac{1}{2}°$ camber angle to be run, while as much as $2\frac{1}{2}°$ camber may be needed on a championship race car fitted with normal road tyres.

The ability of a car to 'turn in' to a corner, rather than plough straight on, is affected by the camber angle. Basically, the more negative camber you add the better the 'turn in', but the more 'twitchy' the car becomes on a straight road; and the tyre's inner edge can get scuffed out quickly if you run too much negative camber, as it gets hot and does all the work. Negative camber is where, looking from the front, the top of the tyre is nearer the car than the bottom of the tyre, or where the wheel leans in at the top. Under hard cornering the car pushes on the tyre, and adding negative camber gets all the tyre working against the ground.

This only really affects the front of a front-wheel-drive car, as the rear simply follows the front and is pulled by it. It's possible to alter the rear camber with tiny shims behind the rear stub axles, but this is not normally needed on road cars.

On a Mk1, simply adjust the offset bolt on the base of the strut to get your desired angle, retighten firmly and recheck. On a Mk2 and 3 there are two possibilities for adjustment; either file the hole a little to slot it and use a slightly turned down bolt, or slide the lower wishbone ball joint in or out to suit. Mk4s have no adjustment, as the slide-in strut has no place to allow movement, and the lower wishbone ball joints are fixed too.

The castor angle, which affects the 'centralising' feel of the steering, is the offset, forwards and backwards, of a line through the front hub where it attaches to the front suspension. Put simply, the greater the castor angle, the stronger the centralising action of the steering, but the heavier it will feel too. As

usual, it's full of compromise, and it's difficult to alter on a VW. The only practical way to add castor is to fit offset top mounts towards the rear of the available hole in the inner wing top to increase the angle of the hub – but this is only for racers.

Correct tracking is essential to avoid excessive tyre wear and to get the best from the suspension. Tracking is the alignment of the front wheels (in this case) forwards. It's the in or out position of one wheel to its opposite number. As you accelerate or brake, the front wheels tend to get pushed rearwards, thus slightly opening the distance up and increasing the tracking. As a consequence the wheels then face outwards and the tendency is for the car to pull slightly outwards too, so we need to allow for this when it's standing still and set the tracking slightly in. Achievement of the necessary accuracy calls for specialist equipment, but special 4-wheel alignment is not normally necessary as the rear is non-adjustable anyway.

Steering racks

Mk1s have a good strong rack in standard form. The common problem on accident damaged cars is cracking of the actual body around the rack mount, so if yours clicks and cracks in use, take the carpets out and inspect the floor for cracks.

High ratio (less turns from lock to lock) internals are available from tuners, but the quality is not very good, and it's really unnecessary, even in competition, as it makes the steering even heavier.

TSR Performance makes a power-steering kit for all the Mk1-based cars, Cabrios and Sciroccos. It uses all the later power-steering pumps, and a special rack and fitting to fit the Mk1. It's ideal for the bigger-wheeled and heavy Cabrios, and weaker Mk1 owners. The rack is a higher ratio (2.7), so less turns from lock to lock.

The Mk2 rack is fine in standard spec. There are two types of actual rack fitted, but both have the same fittings externally. High ratio internals are available, the better one being LHD only!

Power steering is easily retro-fitted as long as you get all the brackets, etc., but not to 1300

Mk2s as the pumps are different. Small-engined cars need to use the pump and brackets from a Seat Ibiza or Polo 1.4. Make sure you have the rack coupling too, as it's different and expensive to buy new from VW.

There is little available for Mk3s and Mk4s.

Wheels and tyres

It's an impossible area to cover, as so much is in the eye of the beholder. Fitting larger diameter and wider wheel/tyre combinations is probably the most common modification carried out on Golfs. There are several points to ponder.

First, apart from the 'look', what are you trying to achieve? 18" alloys may look great but they are a hugely expensive mistake if they give terrible handling and catch the arches on every bump. The early cars' suspension does not work well with tyres over 195/50/15s.

On Mk1s the rear arches will need modifying by bending the outer lip under to give sufficient clearance for even 195/50/15 tyres, and the bumpstop trick will be needed on a lowered car. Even then, a Mk1 with two people in the back will occasionally catch the rear arches on speed bumps and big holes in the road.

Mk2 and 3s are better, up to 17" wheels with 215/40/17 tyres will fit with the same mods as a Mk1.

Mk4s have more room, and these later cars suffer far less with strange handling when larger tyres are fitted

The wider the tyre, the more 'tramlining' will be felt, and they can spoil the good handling and enjoyment. Call me old-fashioned, but the best cars to drive are generally on a conservative-sized rim with a tyre not over 215 in width.

The golden rule with wheel choice is to be very careful with the ET measurement. This is critical if 'bump steer' and fouling of the rear arches are to be avoided. Most VWs use ET35 on wheels up to 16". Beyond that size, consult the wheel dealer, as most good alloys have a fitment guide.

Avoid using other car manufacturers' alloys, e.g. Renault, BMW, etc., as the ET is usually incorrect, and the ring that locates the wheel to the hub will not fit correctly. This ring is sometimes removable and replaceable, so first make sure it's there, and that it's the correct size. It needs to be a firm fit on the centre of the hub, or terrible shake (like incorrect wheel balance) will be felt through the steering.

Earlier cars run a 4 x 100mm bolt pattern (all Mk1s and 2s and the more basic Mk3s), but sporty Mk3s like the GTI and VR6 run 5 x 100mm centres, as do Mk4s.

Cheap alloys often let the air out, and are porous, or lose their lacquer in the first winter weather. Be careful buying second-hand alloys, they are often square rather than round, and the deep dished inside of the wheels is easily bent. Check them by spinning them up on a wheel balancing machine. Alloys can be repaired, and you may want to have this done if you have a classic model and are keen on keeping things strictly original. The cost per rim, though, is normally about the same as new ones.

Avoid wheel spacers, as these normally don't allow the tight fitment of the ring in the alloy wheel to locate properly on the hub. Extended nut multi-fitment spacers are dangerous, and unnecessary if the correct alloy wheels are used in the first place.

There are, however, suitable spacers available from Eibach with a double flange on both sides to correctly locate the wheels. They are available with the correct bolts in 5mm, 10mm and 15mm thicknesses.

Always fit the best possible quality tyres you can afford, though most these days are good quality. Try to avoid so-called 'budget tyres', as some of these are nothing like as safe, especially in wet conditions.

Track days ruin tyres. Try to get a second set of wheels and tyres for sport use and keep your road tyres for the road. Some excellent purpose-made soft track tyres from Yokohama will not last long on the road, but allow you much better on-track performance.

A cheaper alternative for track days is a set of well-scrubbed (worn) road tyres, Toyo being a favourite of mine. You do not want lots of tread for the track, unless its pouring down with rain, in which case use your road tyres instead. In the dry, blow them up hard (over 40psi) and set the balance by altering the rear pressures only – harder for a tail-happy car, softer for more neutral handling.

braking systems

The entire Golf range shares a similar braking system, but there are big differences between the individual cars. From the earliest Mk1s, the cars have been fitted with disc brakes at the front, a servo, and a compensating valve on the rear suspension, and decent rear brakes. Over the years this has been improved on with each new model that has appeared, so uprating to the later systems, where possible, will dramatically improve the braking of earlier models.

Starting from the earliest Mk1 cars, a brief description on the individual models will be beneficial.

The Mk1 1100, 1300 and 1500 models were introduced with 239mm non-vented (solid) discs in original form, with small square-shaped pads in a suitable calliper. The rear brakes were drums with wheel bearings built into the drums, instead of the normal system of separate hubs and drums. This arrangement was lighter, simple and obviously cheaper to produce at the factory, but it means that any drum replacements will also require new wheel bearings to be fitted at the same time. The wheel bearings are taper type, so require careful setting up to avoid seizure or excess sloppiness.

The servo was fitted to assist pedal pressure and improve the 'feel' of the brakes, and a rear beam brake compensator was fitted on most cars except the very basic 1100/1300 models. The idea of the compensator is to prevent locking of the rear brakes under hard braking. More on this later.

The coming of the GTI models required better braking, so the front discs were uprated to 239mm vented discs, with matching callipers. The later callipers have banana-shaped pads. Simply retro-fitting these later callipers and the vented discs will dramatically improve any earlier cars, or lesser models than the GTI. Many early Polos will accept this conversion. VW used the GTI set-up on the quick G40 Polo model. All 239mm conversions fit well with any 13" wheel.

Mk2 standard systems are different in several ways. First, the GTI models were fitted with disc brakes at the rear, but the non-sporty models, diesels and carburettor cars retained the drum brakes of a Mk1, although the handbrake cables were of different length. On the front, the basic models still had the GTI callipers, even with non-vented discs, and the discs were thicker than the Mk1. The calliper was attached to a fixed cast bracket, actually part of the hub, so fitting larger discs is virtually impossible with this type of hub assembly, as it's impossible to move the calliper outwards because of the fixed brackets.

On all but the really early 1300 cars, fitting GTI 239mm vented discs is simply a question of bolting them on. The GTI pads replace the thicker pads of the non-vented cars.

The rear beam compensator was also different in form from a Mk1, but worked the same way. Servos are dealt with at the end of this chapter.

The advent of the 16V Golf brought a better and bigger 256mm disc and a different-shaped calliper with it, but only after 1989. The early cars still ran 239mm normal Mk2 GTI brakes. This later set-up was inherited from the Passat range, and retro-fitting it, including the different hubs, works well on a Mk2. The later callipers are easily spotted because the clips that tension the pads show easily, and the pads are shorter and no longer banana-shaped.

The hubs have different bolt holes for the

The two common pads are (top) 256/280mm pads and (bottom) 239mm pads.

Mk2 lower swivels, the larger power-steering version on the left, and the earlier type on the right.

later calliper, and larger lower mounts for the swivel joints. All cars with power steering have the larger swivel joints.

Rear callipers on the Golfs have been a cause of problems for years. As soon as they get a bit ancient, the handbrake linkage seizes internally. It's virtually impossible to unseize, and replacement units are needed. The later Mk2 from 1989 onwards had slightly different callipers, requiring slightly longer handbrake cables, but these also suffer the same problems. The Mk3 callipers were different again, but still fit the Mk2, and the subsequent Mk4 callipers are alloy, so lighter. These will also bolt on to a Mk2 with the correct rear banjo brake pipes.

Mk3 cars had several brake systems, from the very basic diesels with unbelievably horrible 239mm non-vented discs to the huge 288mm brakes of the last of the VR6 range. Measure

Mk4 rear callipers in alloy with the banjo rear brake pipes to allow fitting to all disc-braked models.

yours and then go as big as you can afford. Most of the sports models – 8V, 16V and VR6 – used the 280mm disc and calliper, until the 288mm set appeared. These were excellent brakes even in standard form.

Mk4 brakes follow the Mk3 in being excellent in standard form, and they share most of the same parts. Skodas and Seats also share these brakes.

Brake modifications – Mk1 models

The Mk1 Golf had quite a name for inefficient brakes, but they are easy to modify and can be made as good as later cars without busting the bank. The most basic improvement is simply changing the front brake pads to higher quality sports material. There are many available – Mintex, Ferodo, EBC and Black Diamond, to name a few. Any good tuner will have several types available, and they will also be advertised in magazines. All pads have their good points, but remember that whatever type you decide to fit they are not at their best straight after fitting. All pads require a bedding down period until they match the discs to which they have been fitted. The discs will need to be in excellent unscored condition too, so inspection is vital before fitting the new pads. New discs are not expensive, so seriously consider replacing them at the same time.

Discs

The standard ex-factory VW 239mm vented disc is of high quality, and some of the cheaper replacement 'quality' discs are nothing like as good. Recently the factory replacement discs have become much cheaper, resulting from a change of policy at VW, so you pay your money and take your choice.

There are many aftermarket performance discs available – slotted, cross drilled and a combination of both. The idea behind the slotting and drilling treatment is to give the gasses and dust created under hard braking an easy escape route. Also, in rain, the water trapped between the disc and the pad can get away easier. The likelihood is that you will decide on the disc treatment for aesthetic reasons. Like alloy wheels, it's largely in the eye of the beholder. All the treatments work better than the plain disc, but the greater the surface treatment (e.g. combination drilled and slotted) the more wear there will be on the disc pad.

Sometimes there will be more noise, too, as the holes and slots cross the pads. For a pad, it's a bit like driving over paving stones at speed.

Larger disc conversions

The diameter of your wheels will dictate the maximum size of discs you can fit to any Golf or derivative. The calliper and disc will need to be able to fit inside the wheel without touching the rims of the wheel. Remember that 13" wheels will be limited to 239mm discs. If your wheels are 14", then 270mm is the largest, and with a 15" or larger wheel 285mm is the maximum because the disc diameter is dictated by the available clearance behind the wheel rim.

Many models of the Mk1, Cabrio, Campaign and Scirocco, have 14" wheels in standard form. Also, 14" steel wheels are cheap and plentiful from Mk2s, and they fit straight onto all models.

TSR Performance has produced a 270mm kit for these cars. It consists of specially made

Mk1 conversion brackets to allow larger discs to be fitted; 270mm on left and 285mm on right.

270mm vented discs from Black Diamond (with either slotted, cross drilled or combination treatment), Pagid sports pads to suit the standard GTI calliper and steel brackets and bolts to allow the calliper to be remounted slightly further away from the hubs. This is a

simple and reliable system with huge benefits to the feel and braking ability of these cars.

Fitting larger discs provides a bigger 'heat sink' area for the generated heat to spread out into and then to escape from. It also gives greater leverage to the callipers as they are now mounted further from the centre of the hub. The extension brackets in the kit move the calliper in towards the centre of the vehicle, thus getting slightly more clearance from the wheel rim, and more air flow to help cool the brakes. The discs have to be specially manufactured to allow for this extra offset of the new bracket.

Because this conversion retains the original calliper and pad size, it is very cost effective, and replaces the parts that would be in need of replacement anyway on a high-mileage vehicle.

With 15" or larger wheels, fit the TSR 285mm kit. Essentially it is a larger disc and different bracket version of the 270mm kit. The

The ultimate replacement disc, drilled and grooved, from Black Diamond. (Black Diamond)

The standard
disc next to the
specially offset
TSR 270/285mm
big disc. This
offset allows for
the special
bracket to fit
neatly.

advantages are the same as before, but more so, as it's larger still.

It is also easy to fit the 256mm 16V Golf Mk2 discs to a Mk1, using the 16V callipers and the calliper carriers from an Audi 80. The bolt holes are different on the 16V calliper, so it won't fit directly without the Audi 80 Quattro carrier. Not surprisingly, the end result is somewhere between a TSR 270mm kit and standard brakes.

Volvo callipers and discs can be used, but it's hardly worth the effort. The only advantage is the cost if using cheap second-hand parts – new, they cost more than VW.

At the rear of a Mk1 the standard drum set-up is fine. It suffers from neglect, though, and often it is well overdue for a rebuild. Once the drum set-up is in good condition you will have excellent brakes, and a superb handbrake, unlike cars with discs fitted at the rear. The downside is the look. Discs look better.

The 16V Scirocco brought the disc conversion at the rear, but on a Mk1 chassis. It

was a rare car (not available here except as imports), but it has the handbrake cable you need to fit a Mk1 with a Mk2 rear disc conversion. The stub axles, discs, callipers and fitting will need to be sourced from a Mk2, and then add two handbrake cables from a 16V Scirocco, and it's virtually complete. You will also need to fit Mk2 flexible brake pipes and suitable steel brake pipes to match the flexible pipes. Bleeding the callipers is difficult (see the Mk2 section). It looks good and will accept fancy rear Mk2 discs to match the front ones you have already fitted.

It's quite possible that you will need to adjust the compensator valve slightly if you fit rear discs, as the rear brakes may lock before the front.

Compensator

As mentioned before, this valve is fitted to the rear axle of most Mk1 cars. The valve recognises the dipping of the front of the car under heavy braking, as it is attached to the rear beam and the car's floor by a spring. When the rear axle drops down the valve is set to cut off the rear brake fluid supply to avoid the unloaded rear brakes locking a wheel and skidding.

It's often the case that the valve is seized, so inspect yours carefully. It has a spring tension adjuster and, as mentioned before, it may require slight adjustment if the car has been lowered or shows signs of locking wheels under heavy braking. It's a sound idea to mark it first before adjustment is attempted, so you can return to the original setting if you find it difficult to get right. It can be very sensitive to adjustment.

There are several aftermarket adjusters, but all need one rear brake line, not the two fitted as standard on a Golf. This is fine on a car used in motorsport, as most are adjustable inside the car to suit the track conditions. Later Cabrios and Sciroccos use a different system. On the pipes leading from the servo towards the rear of the car, but next to the servo, are valves that sense the pressures. These are virtually non-adjustable and rarely need any adjustment.

Replacing the brake lines is covered later in this chapter.

Brake modifications – Mk2 models

The limiting factor with Mk2 brakes is the hub/calliper fitting previously mentioned. The calliper will not unbolt from the hub without leaving the inbuilt cast brackets behind. We used to modify the hubs in the early days of the Mk2 by cutting off the brackets and welding up the centre of the hub, drilling and tapping new holes to accept the brake callipers from a Mk1, and then fitting 285mm discs from the Mk1 kit.

All Mk2s have rear discs except the diesel and carburettor cars. They can be fitted easily from a GTI model.

Although this worked well, it was expensive and difficult, but the coming of the later 16V hubs with completely removable brackets and callipers solved the problem for us. Now we could fit extension brackets and 285mm discs, if required, to 15" and larger wheels.

The G60 Corrado brought an even better standard brake into the equation. They were fitted with a 4-bolt wheel, the same as the normal Golf, and a huge 280mm disc. The calliper was basically the same as the post-1989 16V Golf, but had different calliper brackets to allow for the bigger diameter disc.

This set-up fits onto any 1989 Golf 16V, but will need a later hub and calliper to fit any earlier 16V or all 8V Golfs. This is the ultimate set-up on a Mk2 Golf.

The Mk3 cars are a source of hubs and callipers, but as they are 5-bolt, you also need to change the wheels over. Remember that all 8V Golfs had the cast-in brackets, even the late cars.

To go even bigger with disc sizes requires wheels over 16" to have sufficient clearance for the discs and callipers. There are several ultimate AP Racing kits around 310mm, all these have multi-pot callipers and cost around £1,300.

All the discs are available with cross drilled, slotted or combination form, so choose according to your desire. Fit high-quality pads and your braking problems are at an end. All

A Mk2 with Black Diamond rear discs and Mk4 alloy callipers fitted.

The front of the same Mk2 with 16V 256mm hubs and 280mm G60 brakes fitted. The white marker pen has been used to show that the bolts are all torqued up.

Mk2 servos are excellent and do not require modification.

Brake modifications – Mk3/4 models

These cars have excellent standard brakes, so simply replace the pads and discs with the best possible quality sports set-up, as on the previous cars, and that is all that is needed. AP Racing kits also make ultimate road car conversions, as mentioned before, but a cheaper answer is to fit the superb Seat Ibiza Cupra R front brakes. These fit directly onto the existing hubs, and work brilliantly for far less cost.

Brake fade

Brake fade is a commonly used term to describe brakes that start to feel spongy in hard use. There are many causes of brake fade, some more obvious than others.

First, it can be caused by the front discs and pads exceeding their intended working temperature through misuse or overuse. The effect is a soft feel to the brake pedal, and a horrible sinking feeling in the driver.

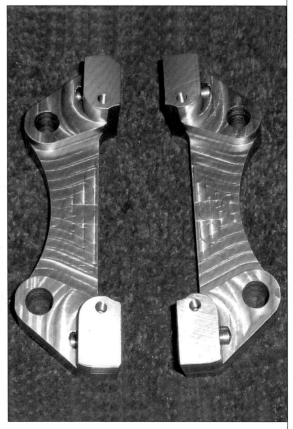

The Seat 305mm mounting brackets to suit the Brembo callipers. This may need extra machining to fit some models.

Brembo 305mm kit as fitted to Seat Ibiza Cupra, ideal for an upgrade on a 280mm car with suitable alloys.

The answer is to fit better materials, especially brake pads with a greater and higher heat range, e.g. good quality sport pads from a well-known producer. Larger discs help, too, as heat dispersal is better than with smaller discs. Good practice after heavy braking is releasing the brakes as soon as you stop, as this allows the heat to come off the discs equally. This is prevented if you hold the brakes on and may give rise to warping.

The second cause of brake fade is poor fluid in the system. Brake fluid absorbs moisture (it's hygroscopic by nature) and if tiny bubbles of water have got into it, then braking pressure will compress them, giving a 'mushy' feel. Any water in the system will also corrode the brake pipes from the inside. Using high-quality brake fluid and changing it every two to three years will keep your brakes in uncorroded good condition.

Here are a few hints:

DO NOT pump the brake pedal on an older car to bleed the brakes. It will almost certainly ruin the master cylinder seals, as during the pumping you will push the master cylinder seals into the unused but dirty part of the cylinder. That will require the fitting of a new master cylinder to cure it. Simply buy a low-pressure bleed unit that often uses a tyre to supply the pressure. They are cheaper than a new master cylinder and easier to use too, as bleeding becomes a one man task.

If you have problems bleeding rear callipers, try removing them one at a time and holding them bleed nipple upwards. Also make sure the rear beam is not hanging down, or the compensator will cut off the supply, thinking the car is braking hard!

Do not let the callipers hang down on their brake pipes when working on the brakes. Brake pipes are not strong enough to support the weight of the cast-iron callipers.

Always drill out and retap any broken set screws if they break off while removing the front discs, as they locate the discs, and make changing a wheel so much easier on a dark wet night. Without them, the disc is loose as soon as the wheel bolts are removed, and free to turn, making refitting of the wheel difficult.

On later Mk3 and Corrado rear beams the rear compensator is virtually impossible to remove, as the steel securing bolts go through the alloy compensator. They corrode very badly where the two metals react, and you will need to replace the compensator if this has happened.

Inspect the rubber front brake pipes very carefully where they are held onto the strut. I have seen badly rubbed through pipes here, as they chafe all the time.

Brake hoses

The rubber brake hoses are well worth replacing with Aeroquip/Goodrich, or equivalent, steel-braided hoses. They are cheap when bought in sets, easy to replace and will

Mk2 rear brake compensator before years of grime and mud make it very scruffy.

greatly improve the feel of a car's brakes.

Standard rubber hoses have a limited lifespan because the rubber deteriorates with use, and when they are old they expand and lose effective pressure when you brake. Fitting the braided brake lines also forces you to change your brake fluid, and that's a good thing. The kits are available in car types, but you need to tell the tuning shop if you have rear discs fitted

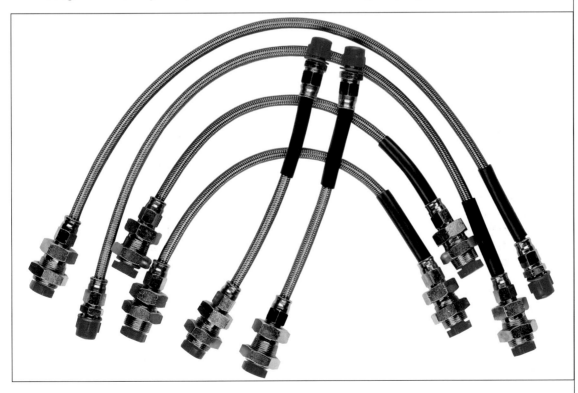

Aircraft quality brake lines are essential for improving the feel of the brake pedal. (Black Diamond)

Master cylinders: Mk1 (left) and bigger 22mm version that suits the larger Mk2 servo. Note the different fittings; the 22mm cylinder needs the correct reservoir and modified pipes.

A Mk2 servo.

to a Mk1, for example. Later VR6 and Mk4 cars have banjo calliper fittings, instead of the more common screw-in fitting, so take a look before ordering. During final tightening do not twist the braided lines as this causes internal damage, and it's impossible to spot externally.

Master cylinders and servos

The only model Golf to benefit from a bigger master cylinder is the Mk1, when fitted with a bigger servo from a Mk2. The Passat 22mm unit also fits well, but will require modifications to the brake pipes. Some people fit this cylinder to the Mk2s but it's not really necessary.

The Mk1 also benefits from a Mk2 servo, as the Mk2 has a 3:1 servo against Mk1's 2:1 servo.

Remember, all the servo does is to apply pressure to the master cylinder to help you brake, it's like a lever. It stands to reason that the later servos help more than the Mk1 servos,

Mk2 servo fitted with 22mm master cylinder to uprate an under-servoed Mk1.

so the brakes will feel as if they are better, with less pedal effort to achieve the same stopping powers.

Don't muddle up the feel from the reality. The brakes are no better in mechanical terms, they simply feel better. If you drive a modern car as well as an early Golf, then it's most noticeable, as it's an area that has improved greatly in recent years. Bear in mind that the Golf Mk1 is an old design now.

Safety first

You should not work on your brakes unless you are a capable and competent mechanically minded person.

Be careful with brake dust, and do not blow it off a brake component by mouth or air line. Use an aerosol brake protector and then wipe off the dust.

Brake fluid absorbs moisture from the atmosphere so, if you are storing it, use an airtight container and keep it for no longer than two years.

Brake fluid will severely mark paint if it comes in contact with it, so take extra care with cloths containing traces of brake fluid.

It's a sound idea to wear thin rubber gloves when dealing with brake fluid.

Three-way pipe fittings required if the later master cylinder and servo from a Mk2 are fitted to a Mk1.

06 some of my favourite cars

my favourites

This book has been written for enthusiastic Golf owners, and with a definite emphasis on mechanical rather than body modifications. This is not to say, though, that a mixture of the two cannot be very effective, and as the Golf has been with us now for over 30 years, virtually everything possible has been modified before by someone, somewhere.

The cars described here are those that I have known and been impressed by for one reason or another. I apologise for the bias towards the Mk1, but it's simply the most dynamic of the whole Golf family, and certainly it is the fastest for the least cost.

Mk1s

One of the most long-lasting Mk1s was OKU 968 X, my own development car. It was originally a 1600 GTI, but we initially fitted an 1800 engine with a TSR cam and head for the owner back in the late 1980s. He lost his licence almost immediately! We bought the GTI back from his dad, and kept it for 11 years.

As the TSR Performance demonstrator, it did 160,000 miles and was driven by most of the country. Every weekend in the season it was competing in hillclimbs and sprints, shows and quarter-mile runs. Its body was totally unmodified to allow it to run in the road car class in competition, and because I like standard-looking cars with lots of power!

'OKU', my faithful GTI for 10 years, testbed for TSR Performance products, in this case saving tyre wear at a hillclimb.

Engine

A fully balanced 1800 GTI Mk1 8V unit fitted with a 'Pack D' race head (35/40.5mm valves), standard pistons and rods.
TSR 103 solid cam, vernier cam pulley from Kent.
Polished inlet manifold with Audi throttle body modified linkage.
Standard distributor and ignition.
Basically standard injection based on the early 1600 metering head, as it's best for fuelling.
JR panel filter in drilled air box, with inlet pipe replaced by an alloy tube.
Late Mk1 radiator and header tank, original oil cooler.
Ansa four-into-one exhaust manifold and Jetex system.

147bhp at the wheels, 170bhp at the flywheel, 0–60 in 6.5 sec.

Transmission

Lightened 210mm flywheel, Black Diamond heavy-duty clutch.
A rare Italian 5-speed gear cluster with an ultra close ratio straight cut gearset and a 55mph first gear! Fifth gear could be changed for different events.
A Quaife limited-slip differential was the most important part fitted for traction.

Brakes

Front were standard-sized 239mm Black Diamond with Pagid pads. Rear standard. Standard servo and linkage set-up, carefully adjusted.

Suspension

All sorts were tried, but the best set-up was found to be the Koni dampers and Koni springs from the original kits. They suited the sudden camber changes on hillclimbs and were easy to set up. Coil-over kits were not available when this car was active.
Eibach anti-roll bars, front and rear.
Poly rack bushes.

Wheels and tyres

Steel 14" wheels and 186/60/14 Bridgestone hillclimb tyres. The class only allows 14" rims.

Interior

Apart from a BBS steering wheel and a full harness it was original.
A nice postscript is that this demo car spawned many others! The Mk1 of Andrew James is exactly the same spec and was built ten years after he drove OKU, after he had saved up a bit of money! It is regularly used in competition, and still is very competitive.

Now a radical Mk1 from Graham Vanstone in north Devon. This particular car is a regular winner of our rolling road shoot outs at TSR. It climbs out of the rollers and needs several brave, or foolish, people to sit on the front panel to restrain the beast. It is an interesting road racer format, and remains just road legal. The finish and care taken on this car is superb.

Engine

20V 2-litre, with JE pistons, steel rods, ARP bolts. This contains a special crank and fully gas-flowed head with special attention to the valves.
Crane billet cams in steel.
HOR technology cam caps in titanium with special springs.
Specially fabricated exhaust manifold and system.
Custom radiator.

208bhp at the wheels, 240bhp at the engine.

Injection

Fully throttle body and MBE management to suit, custom loom.
ITG filter positioned either in front headlight for max cold air or inside the engine bay for road legal situations.

Transmission

020 gearbox with lower final drive.
Quaife limited-slip differential.
Special rose-jointed linkage for gearchange.
Helix paddle clutch on lightened flywheel.

Suspension

Leda coil-overs, adjustable.
Eibach front anti-roll bar and Neuspeed rear.
Lower brace from 16V Scirocco, top brace welded between turrets.
Alloy rack bushes.
Sorg camber/castor adjustable top mounts in alloy.

Graham Vanstone's ultimate MK1 – note the huge air filter in the 'track day' position in place of the headlight.

A 2-litre 20V on aftermarket injection, producing 240bhp. Note the alloy suspension top mounts to increase caster.

The last thing a
bug sees!

OK, what's
under the
cover? Throttle
bodies!

Brakes

310mm front with callipers and brackets to suit.
Rear Mk4 callipers and Mk2 discs.
Specially-built bias twin cylinders in the car
with Aeroqip lines and adjustment front
to rear.

Bodyshell

Based on a 1983 shell, fully internally painted
and lightened as much as possible. Glass fibre
bonnet and hatch. No trim!
Stack rev counter and carbon-fibre accessories,
such as spare wheel cover.
Roll Centre cage fully fitted.

Wheels and tyres

Compomotive alloys fitted with Yokohama A048.

Detail art! The
carbon fibre
spare wheel
cover.

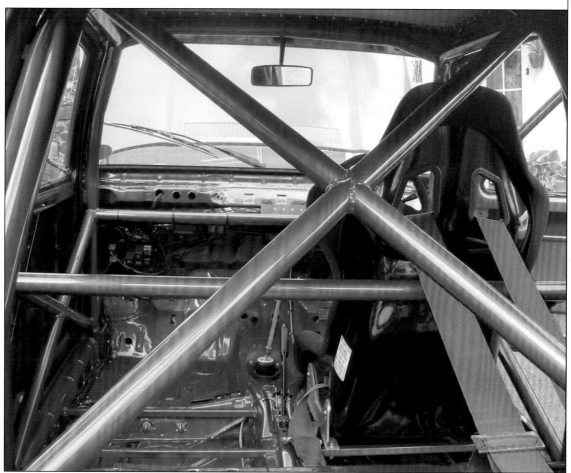

It's a bit of a
racer!

Mk2s

This particular car is a good example of a Mk2 16V 'sleeper', or innocent car with well-modified mechanics. It was originally owned by a health visitor in Woking, but now by Ian Bartlett. He acquired it with 91K, complete with factory alloy wheels and a full history. The Koni kit was fitted early on and a Remus exhaust system was added when the old one finally needed replacement. The car has featured in several VW magazines over the years.

The 1800 16V was originally fitted with a TSR 'Pack A' head and stainless exhaust manifold, and gave 150bhp at the wheels, but later a TSR 2-litre block was fitted under the head.

This car is regularly seen at most track days, but gets Ian to work during the week, and is an ideal road/competition spec car still suitable for everyday use.

Engine

Now a TSR 2-litre block with full balancing, TSR 'Pack A' head.
Schrick 268 inlet cam and 276 exhaust cam.

161bhp at wheels, 202bhp at engine at 6,750rpm, 160lb ft at 6,520rpm. (Figures: Stealth Racing)

Transmission

16V standard gearbox with Quaife limited-slip differential fitted.
Lightened flywheel and heavy-duty clutch.

Injection

Basically standard 16V with Stealth modified warm-up valve.

Ian Bartlett's Mk2 16V, a 'sleeper' if ever there was one.

Suspension

Top adjustable Koni dampers and Eibach springs.
Eibach anti-roll bars.
Poly bushes

Brakes

256mm discs and Pagid pads, but a 280mm set is ready to fit. Rears as standard.

Wheels and tyres

Original BBS (G60) alloys fitted with Toyo 195/50/15 tyres. Track tyres are Dunlop Formula R inter.

Interior

Basically standard, but fitted with a new steering wheel and Recaro driver's seat, and full harness for track days.

The Momo steering wheel.

H909 CFJ

Well Officer, it's totally standard!

other books from Haynes Publishing

**You & Your
VW Golf GTI**
Buying, enjoying,
maintaining, modifying
by Andy Butler
ISBN 1 85960 810 8
£17.99

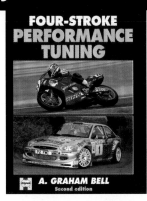

**Four-Stroke
Performance Tuning
(2nd Edition)**
by A. Graham Bell
ISBN 1 85960 435 8
£17.99

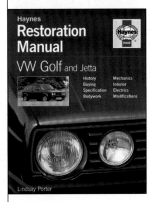

**VW Golf and Jetta
Restoration Manual**
by Lindsay Porter
ISBN 1 85960 448 X
£17.99

**Race and Rally Car
Source Book
(4th Edition)**
The guide to building
or modifying a
competition car
by Allan Staniforth
ISBN 1 85960 846 9
£19.99

**Improve & Modify
Golf & Jetta (inc GTI)
(Re-issue)**
by Lindsay Porter and
Dave Pollard
ISBN 0 85429 748 0
£19.99

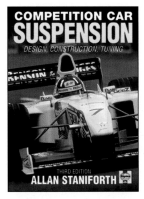

**Competition Car
Suspension
(3rd Edition)**
Design, construction
and tuning
by Allan Staniforth
ISBN 1 85960 644 X
£19.99

Engine Management
Optimising
carburettors, fuel
injection and ignition
systems
By Dave Walker
ISBN 1 85960 835 3
£17.99

Birth of the Beetle
The development of
the Volkswagen by
Ferdinand Porsche
by Chris Barber
ISBN 1 85960 959 7
£30.00